STARTING NOW

COLLEGE IS HARD - THIS CAN HELP

A 30-day guide to becoming
who you want to be in college

Crystal Chiang and Gerald Fadayomi

STARTING NOW

Published by Orange, a division of The reThink Group, Inc.

5870 Charlotte Lane, Suite 300

Cumming, GA 30040 U.S.A.

The Orange logo is a registered trademark of The reThink Group, Inc.

All Scripture quotations, unless otherwise noted, are taken from the Holy Bible, New International Version®. NIV®. Copyright © 1973, 1978, 1984 by International Bible Society. Used by permission of Zondervan.

Other Orange products are available online and direct from the publisher. Visit our website at www.WhatIsOrange.org for more resources like these.

ISBN: 978-1-63570-090-9

Authors: Crystal Chiang & Gerald Fadayomi

Lead Editor: Sarah Anderson

Art Direction: Nate Brandt

Project Manager: Nate Brandt

Printed in the United States of America

First Edition 2019

2 3 4 5 6 7 8 9 10 11

05/16/19

WHERE DO I START?

STARTING NOW was designed specifically for starting *after* you've arrived at college.

If you're still in high school (yes, even if you're taking a few college courses online) or are waiting for your college classes to start over the summer, put this book down for now and pick it up again on the first day of college.

If you're already in college, go ahead and turn the page. No matter what point it is in the semester, you're ready to get started right now!

TABLE OF **CONTENTS**

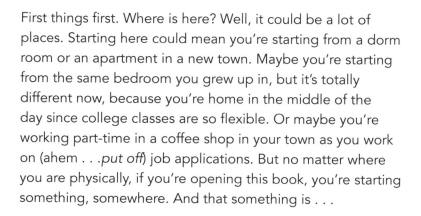

START HERE

First things first. Where is here? Well, it could be a lot of places. Starting here could mean you're starting from a dorm room or an apartment in a new town. Maybe you're starting from the same bedroom you grew up in, but it's totally different now, because you're home in the middle of the day since college classes are so flexible. Or maybe you're working part-time in a coffee shop in your town as you work on (ahem . . .*put off*) job applications. But no matter where you are physically, if you're opening this book, you're starting something, somewhere. And that something is . . .

the beginning of adult life.

Okay, maybe you don't feel like an adult because you're wearing a hoodie you got in middle school, you have exactly four dollars in your bank account, and you still sleep with a retainer. That's fair. But the truth is, regardless of how you feel, you are closer to adult-ing than ever before. Chances are, if you're reading this, high school is somewhere in the rear view and life is going to look a little bit different than it ever has mostly because . . .

you're in charge.

Well . . .sort of. It's possible you thought you would be more in charge than you actually are. In fact, you might be surprised at how little freedom you have and how much your parents or your school or your coaches still manage what you do. Maybe you still have a curfew, a spending allowance, and somebody telling you to eat your veggies and go to bed. Or, it's possible you're shocked at the amount of freedom and responsibility you've been given. Be in charge of your own schedule? Your own budget? Your own academic life? Is that even a good idea?!?

Whether you feel like you haven't been given enough freedom or you've been given too much too soon, the truth is *you are here*. You are at the beginning of something entirely new. As an adult, you've been handed (or you're in the process of getting) the keys to your own life.

And now the question is . . .

where are you going?

And if you're honest, that question is both exciting and terrifying. That's okay, because here's something that most people won't tell you. *Nobody has any idea.* Your friends don't know—even if they act like they do. Your parents didn't know at your age, and they may still not be sure. That's because "where are you going?" is a big question with a lot of potential answers. So how do you know you're going the right way? Especially now? At the beginning? When you sit in the driver's seat of your own life, how do you know you're headed in the right direction?

There are a lot of ways to answer that,
but let's start with one:

Spend more time focused on a "WHO" not a "DO".

Here's what we mean. When thinking about where they're headed in college or in life—most people think about what they will DO. Maybe you've been asked the question (a thousand times), "what are you going to DO now that you've graduated high school?" Or, "what's your major?"

Or, "what's next?" Most of the time, when people ask that question, they're asking about your future career. That's not a bad thing. But is it the most important thing? Maybe not. Think about this:

The average American now holds six different jobs between the ages of 18 to 26, and two-thirds of these jobs occur between ages 18 and 22.[1]

That means you'll likely change jobs and even career fields more in your lifetime than any generation in history. On top of that, because technology changes so quickly (and because when technology changes, culture does to) there's a good chance your eventual career hasn't even been invented yet.[2]

That's not meant to stress you out. The point is, while work is important, while jobs (and classes that eventually lead to those jobs) are necessary, there may be something else you need to consider—something else that needs to be your primary focus, something that matters now, tomorrow, and ten years from now, no matter what your career ends up being.

We're talking about WHO you are.

What kind of person will you be?

- What kind of son or daughter?

- What kind of boyfriend or girlfriend?

- What kind of student, employee, leader, follower do you want to be?

- How do you hope people describe you?

- What do you want to be true about you six weeks from now or six years from now?

Those are important questions because YOU will take YOU . . .

- into every job
- every relationship and
- every life-situation you have.

In other words, when it comes to aiming your life in the right direction . . .

Who You Are > What You Do.

List words you want to be true about you in college.

....

....

....

List things you want to be known for or want others to say about you.

....

....

....

What do you imagine God wants for you? List a few ways He may want to use you in the world around you.

....

....

....

Maybe you look at that list and it gets you excited about what's to come in the next few years and what you can do to actually grow into the person you want to be. And maybe you look at this list totally overwhelmed—like, "That sounds great, but there's no way I can get there."

Either way, there's good news.

You have a chance to become the kind of person you want to be.

And then . . .

you have another chance
and another one
and another.

Because becoming the WHO you want to be is something you can make a decision to do every. single. day. You can get it wrong one day and wake up the next with a fresh start. You can crush it for the first six months and spend the next three struggling and you still haven't ruined your chances of becoming who you want to be because you are beginning a journey. And it's never too late to start a journey—or start again.

So no matter what you decide about who you want to be, each day is a new opportunity to start becoming that person. Each day is a chance to look in the mirror and say, "Starting today I will . . . "

And that's what this book is about . . .

Deciding for yourself what you will do and who you will be

Every
Single
Day

STARTING NOW

COMMUNITY

WEEK 01

community

[kuh-**myoo**-ni-tee]

Definition: The people you complain to about your Lit class, your weird roommate, or the smell coming from washing machine number 4 in the dorm. (Seriously, don't use that washer).

Definition: The people in your car on a midnight run to Taco Bell during finals week.

Definition: The people on your hall, in your apartment, on your intramural bowling team, or in your classes that you hang out with because you *want* to, not because you have to.

Definition: The people you talk with about life and school and dating and family and faith and all the other stuff that matters.

Definition: The people that will make this whole college experience worth it. *Your* people. The people you will go find . . . starting now.

DAY 1

Have you ever tried to use something in a way OTHER than how it was intended? If you haven't yet, you're sure to do it soon. College is famous for teaching you the magical art of *improvising*. Like you'll forget to do laundry and have to use a t-shirt as a towel. Or in a moment of late-night desperation, you'll explore how to make mac and cheese in the coffee pot. Or due to a malfunctioning microwave, you'll try to use your hair dryer as a hot-pocket warming system.
(*Note*: we don't recommend this.)

At some point you're going to need to improvise. And when it works, it's amazing! But at the same time, nearly everything works *better* when you use it as it was *designed* to be used. That's true of your phone, your microwave, your car . . . and it's true of you.

You were designed for certain conditions. Food, water, shelter, and a steady stream of caffeine all seem to make you work better. And, if you don't have enough of any of those, you feel it. Those are the obvious ones, but they aren't all you need.

Make a list of a few things you can't function without.

....

....

In addition to food, water, and Doritos, from the very beginning, God designed people to need other people. In the beginning, God created everything, and after making the Heavens, the Earth, the sky, the water, the animals, the flowers, the author of Genesis reminds us that all of it was good . . . right up until it wasn't.

> *The LORD God said, "It is not good*
> *for the man to be alone"*
> *(Genesis 2:18a NIV)*

Have you ever thought about that? **The first not-good thing in creation wasn't an earthquake or a fire or an angry porcupine. It was alone-ness.**

Maybe that seems kind of dramatic. After all, there are a LOT worse things in life than being on your own. (Plenty of people have survived a Friday night by themselves.) But it's not ideal. While we may enjoy some time to ourselves we want that to be our choice. While we may like some alone-time, we weren't made to be alone all the time. And God knew that. He knew that even though we can survive being on our own for a little while, it's not how He designed us to live. We weren't made to do life on our own for long. And when we try, just like when we try to go without food or water, we don't function as well as we could.

And that need for other people isn't a design flaw, it's actually part of the original design. Here's what we mean:

> *So God created mankind in his own image,*
> ***in** the **image** of God he created them;*
> *male and female he created them*
> *(Genesis 1:28 NIV emphasis added)*

People, **ALL** people, were created in the image of God, meaning we have some of His attributes. Part of **HIM** is reflected in **US**. And, God Himself is the perfect picture of connection.

Think about it: God, the Father, Jesus (or the son of God), and the Holy Spirit exist *constantly* connected, *constantly* communicating, *constantly* in relationship. So it makes sense if we were created in His image, then we were designed to live the same way. In other words . . .

You were created for connection.

But knowing that isn't the problem. The problem can be finding other people to be connected *with*—especially after you graduate high school. You may not be around the same people you've known since kindergarten. Or, if you are, they may *act* like completely different people now. Or maybe all the different schedules people have make it harder to consistently see the same people often enough to connect with them.

Whatever the reason, **finding your people may not come as easily as it always has.** It may take some *intentionality* on your part. It may take more time and more effort than you expected. *That's okay.* Good things usually do. And while there are a lot of things competing for your attention, one of the best things you will do for yourself as an adult is deciding to do life with other people. In other words,

get serious about getting connected . . .

Starting Now.

Because sometimes good things just happen like . . .

> You find 20 bucks in the console of your car.
>
> You ace a test even when you skipped class and didn't study.
>
> Your Taco Bell drive-thru bag has an extra chalupa inside.

But most of the time, the best things in life take some planning and effort. It's true academically. It's true athletically. And it's definitely true socially. You could get lucky and have the perfect roommate who ends up being in your wedding, or you could end up sitting in class next to your life long best friend, but do you really want to leave that up to chance? Probably not.

So when it comes to finding your people, you may need a plan.

Use the questions below as a guide to help you think through *how, when,* and *where* you will find your people this year.

What kind of people are YOUR people? In other words, what characteristics do you look for in a friend? What kind of people do you enjoy hanging out with?

....

....

....

....

Where could you potentially meet some new people this week?

....

....

....

....

Maybe you *love* meeting new people. Or, maybe it makes you a little nervous. Either way, one of the quickest ways to connect with another person is to ask questions.

What are one or two questions you can ask someone you meet this week that might help you get to know them better? (hint: think background, sports, activities, future plans.)

....

....

....

....

Then, pray. Ask God to help you find the right people for you because . . .

You were created for connection.

22

Let's start with a question.

How did you get here?

Specifically, what made you decide on *this* school?

Maybe, for you, it was an issue of your major and this school offered what you were interested in doing in the future. Maybe it was the athletic program you were drawn to. Maybe your decision was financial—scholarships and in-state tuition helped make the decision for you. Maybe you knew someone who went here and they seemed happy enough so, why not? Or maybe it was something else entirely.

Whatever criteria you used to make that decision, it was probably something pretty important to you. It's something you felt would make your college-life or even your after-college life way better.

Whatever it was, there's something else that also has the power to make or break your college experience, that has the power to influence where you are going and where you end up. More than grades, majors, academics or finances, there's one decision that can impact the next four years (and a lot of years after that) more than anything else. And that's . . .

Friends.

Whether you have a ton of friends already or whether you'd give anything to have just one person to hang out with right now, one thing is true: in this phase of life your friends matter. Who you pick to be by your side for the next few years will effect you now and they will help shape who you become later. And that's good news because you have more control now than ever when it comes to who you pick as friends—which means you have something in common with an ancient king of Israel, Solomon.*

In ancient Israel, Solomon was known as "the wisest person who ever lived". And in all of his wisdom Solomon speaks into the area of friendships, saying the company you keep is vital as you identify the people you do life with in this season. Solomon wrote this:

Walk with the wise and become wise, for a companion of fools suffers harm.
(Proverb 13:20 NIV)

Basically, the people you spend time around—good or bad—have an effect on you. They influence you. That doesn't mean you'll end up exactly like them, but it does mean you will start to resemble them in some ways. Spend enough time with people who are wise and you'll grow more wise. Hang around people who consistently make bad decisions, you'll probably end up making more bad decisions (or at least suffering the fallout from them) as well.

In other words . . .

People who walk together often, end up in the same place.

---

* The son of King David, Solomon was one of Israel's most famous kings. Many of his famous sayings were collected in various books of the Bible. The book of Proverbs is most famous for it's wise sayings and most of those are attributed to Solomon, written from an older man to a younger man learning to find his way in the world.

So at the start of this new stage of life, in this new place, the question, when it comes it your friends, is not so much, *who* do you want to be your friend, but instead: **where do you want to go?**

Start with that question. Because the people you are around will either help you or hurt you in getting there. They will either be bridges or barriers to you becoming the person you ultimately want to become. But bigger than that, they will play a major role in helping you become who God ultimately wants you to become.

So think about what you want to be true about you when you graduate in four (or, let's be honest, five) years. In fact, turn back to page 10 and look at your answers.

If these things represent who you want to become, you're going to want to hang around people who reflect the same characteristics in themselves, and encourage them in you. With that in mind, use the space below to make some decisions about the character traits of people you will hang out with this year.

The people I spend time with must be:

....

....

....

....

The people I spend time with absolutely can NOT be:

....

....

....

....

At the start of this new chapter in your life, you will probably meet a lot of new people. As you do, use the list above like a filter for what kind of roles each of these people should play in your life. Ask yourself who should be an acquaintance and who has the potential to be a friend you spend quality time around, allowing them to influence you in big and small ways.

Now, just so we're clear, people who don't fit those characteristics are not terrible people. In fact, you'll probably meet a lot of really good people this year who may not fit the categories you defined above. That's because this isn't about being a GOOD person. It's about someone being GOOD FOR YOU. And you owe it to yourself as a mature person to decide who will have the kind of access to you that allows influence over you. So much of this year (and the rest of your college years) will be determined by who you spend it with, but don't just settle for *any* people who come along. Instead,

prioritize finding your people.

Prioritize
finding
your
people.

Which one are you?

Introvert   **Extrovert**   **I don't know!**

If you aren't sure, put this book down and go take a quick quiz online to help you find out. (An introvert tends to be energized by spending time alone, and an extrovert enjoys spending more time with people.) Knowing this about how you are wired matters because the more you know about yourself—including how you best relate to people—the better you will be at college life.

Whether you are energized by a crowd or need a nap just thinking about a crowd, one thing is true:

we all need people.

Maybe you need them in small doses, and in small circles. Or maybe you need all people all the time and can never have enough. But no matter how you were made, something doesn't feel right when you're away from people for too long. And that can make college (or any new phase of life) kind of complicated. Because the people who have always been around aren't necessarily around anymore.

That doesn't have to be a bad thing. One of the most exciting parts about this new stage of life is how many new people you will meet. In fact, it's possible some of the people you meet this year will be the very same people who . . .

- are part of some of your favorite memories in the next few years.

- become future roomates.

- cheer you on as you graduate.

- stand beside you at your wedding.

- become your life-long friends.

(Cue sappy music.)

But building those kind of close, authentic, and meaningful friendships takes time. As in *years* potentially . . . not weeks. And that means between now and then you may feel disconnected or maybe even a little lonely.

If you've ever felt alone, or if you're feeling that way right now, that's *perfectly normal. You're* normal. You aren't the first to feel this way. In Psalm 139, David* writes,

> *Where can I go from your Spirit? Where can I flee from your presence? If I go up to the heavens, you are there; if I make my bed in the depths, you are there. If I rise on the wings of the dawn, if I settle on the far side of the sea, even there your hand will guide me, your right hand will hold me fast.*
> *(Psalm 139:7-10 NIV)*

---

*David is the guy you might remember from when you were a kid—and the father of Solomon, who we talked about yesterday. He started out as a shepherd until the prophet Samuel came and told him he would be the next king. The whole becoming king part took a while, but in the meantime, he earned quite the following by defeating the giant Goliath with a stone and sling shot.

You could sum up David's writing this way:

God is everywhere.
God knows everything.
God is with you.

No matter how alone or isolated you may feel there is no corner on the planet that is outside of God's reach. He is with you every step of the way. That's good news. And what's even better, is we have more proof than David did at the time he wrote this. God ultimately gave us Jesus to come to Earth, walk alongside the humanity He made, experiencing the hurt and difficulty being human brings with it. He did it so there could be no question: God is willing to do *anything* to let us know He's with us.

We may not know what prompted David to write what he did, but it's possible he knew exactly what it felt like to be isolated and alone, and that he wrote what he did as a reminder to himself—that even when feeling the most lonely, God was there too.

The same is true for you.

Your friends may be far, but because of Jesus, God is not.

Your family may be distant, but He never will be.

The new friends you had hoped for may be far in the future, but God is with you right now.

Even when you feel lonely,
He will never leave you alone.

Think of where you spend most of your time right now. Maybe it's in class. Maybe a dorm or an apartment. Maybe it's a new town or maybe it's a coffee shop in the same town. With those places in mind, fill in the blanks to personalize David's psalm on the next page.

Where can I go from your Spirit?

Where can I flee from your presence?

If I go to ....,

you are there; if I make my bed in

..., you are there.

If I ...., if I settle (in)

*..., **even there** your*

hand will guide me, your right hand will hold me fast.
(Psalm 139:7-10 NIV emphasis added)

It's possible you don't feel lonely right now, but at some point in this time of change and transition it's bound to happen. When it does, memorize the verse above—not David's version, but yours. And let this truth carry you through: **Even if you feel lonely, He will never leave you alone.**

Spend a few minutes praying and asking God to help you *feel* His presence during times when you may be likely to feel lonely this semester.

Even when you feel lonely, He will never leave you alone.

Have you ever walked into a classroom, sat down, and then realized, five or ten minutes later, you are in the *wrong class*? It's humiliating. Even if you have never done that, that feeling of being a little disoriented in a new place is familiar to everyone. Maybe you have literally gotten lost in a new school building or a new side of town. Or maybe you just feel a little disoriented in a stage of life where almost everything seems new.

The feeling of learning something new when you're more familiar with the way things *used* to be is something early Christians who had grown up in the Jewish faith and culture would have known. For them, becoming a Christ-follower meant redefining thousands of years of belief and tradition. It meant, in some cases, going from a place of relative safety to being in physical danger. Following Jesus meant being in completely new territory. And, like you're probably figuring out, with new territory comes new challenges. Challenges that can make the journey exhausting, challenges that can make you want to give up, challenges that may make you want to pack up your dorm, get on a bus, and head back home for good.

In the New Testament, the writer of the book of Hebrews*
gives us some insight into something that can be helpful for
how to survive in these new situations.

*Let us hold unswervingly to the hope we profess,
for he who promised is faithful. And let us
consider how we may spur one another on
toward love and good deeds . . .
(Hebrews 13:23-24 NIV)*

When we're in a new or stressful situation, we all have a
tendency to become hyper-focused on ourselves, to isolate
ourselves, to retreat into our minds, and withdraw from other
people. But the author of Hebrews is saying, when tempted
to run away, we should actually do the opposite. We should
run in the direction of other people. Notice the use of "us"
and "we". To hold on to hope we need help. We need
people in our corner reminding us of the goodness of God.
Encouraging us to keep going. Pushing us to keep fighting.

The start of college or adult life can be disorienting for just
about anybody. And as overwhelming as it feels, it can be
tempting to forget you are swimming in a sea of people
going through the same thing.

You are surrounded by people who need encouragement,
need friends, need plans this weekend, need hope that it's
going to turn out okay—even if they (or their social media
accounts) don't look like it. In other words . . .

**You're surrounded by people who need someone, just
like you do.**

---

* The book of Hebrews is a distinctly Jewish sounding book. It's obvious from the way the author
writes that the audience was Jewish Christians trying to figure out how these two different parts of
their identity fit together. And fun fact: no one knows who wrote the book of Hebrews. But early
church leaders were so confident that the message on its pages was important for the early church,
they included it in the Bible.

But when you are in a new place and around new people, that's easier said than done. So the writer of Hebrews keeps going.

> *Let us hold unswervingly to the hope we profess, for he who promised is faithful. And let us consider how we may spur one another on toward love and good deeds, **not giving up meeting together, as some are in the habit of doing**, but encouraging one another—and all the more as you see the Day approaching.*
> *(Hebrews 13:23-25 NIV emphasis added)*

When we are tempted to isolate, the writer says to do the opposite. In other words,

don't give up on showing up.

Chances are "the meeting" with other believers may look different for you now than it did just a few years ago. Maybe your parents dragged you to church in high school and you couldn't wait to get out of there. Or, maybe you LOVED your youth group and you're wondering how to recreate that in this new stage of life. Either way, as an adult, one of the things you will decide for yourself is if, when, and *how* you will meet with other followers of Jesus.

In the space on the next page, make a list of organizations on campus (or near campus) where you can meet with other believers. If you aren't sure, do a quick search for your school name and "Christian organization" or "college ministry" and choose a few you'd like to try.

NAME	MEETING PLACE	MEETING TIME
....	....	....
....	....	....
....	....	....

Even if you have tons of Christian organizations on campus, **one of the best ways to meet with other Jesus-followers is to be involved in a local church**. A local church gives you the opportunity to worship with people in different life-stages than you, and that's really important. There will be times over the next few years you may need the advice or encouragement of someone a little older, or you may want to begin to serve someone younger in some way.

Maybe at this stage of life, you'll continue to attend the church you've always attended. Maybe it's time to try somewhere new. Either way, **don't give up on showing up.**

In the space below, write a few characteristics of a church that are important to you. (For example, worship style, opportunities to serve, beliefs, small groups, etc.)

....

....

....

....

One of the best ways to achieve a goal is to SET a goal. **Decide for yourself how many times you will meet with other followers of Jesus this semester.**

....

Don't give up on showing up.

What are some things you do really well? (It's okay. Nobody's reading this but you. Go ahead and brag on yourself for a minute.)

I'm pretty good at:

....

....

....

Now think about who helped you develop that skill. Maybe you're one of the lucky 0.01% of people born with a natural knack for music or basketball or calculus. But most of us, if we are good at anything, got good because somebody along the way helped us out.

A good coach or a mentor can act like rocket fuel on just about any skill you have. In the United States alone, people spend $6 billion[3] every year for coaching on everything from baking to business, to swimming, to dating. And while the coaching *industry* is a relatively new idea, the practice of coaching has been around for a long time.

In the earliest days of Christianity, the Apostle Paul acted as a coach to several young leaders in different cities. Because some of his letters to a certain leader, Timothy, have been preserved, we get to see a little of why and how that relationship worked.

> *I remember your genuine faith, for you share*
> *the faith that first filled your grandmother Lois*
> *and your mother, Eunice. And I know that same*
> *faith continues strong in you. This is why I remind you*
> *to fan into flames the spiritual gift God gave*
> *you when I laid my hands on you. For God has*
> *not given us a spirit of fear and timidity, but of*
> *power, love, and self-discipline.*
> *(2 Timothy1:5-7 NIV)*

In other words, Paul writes to Timothy, I know where you come from. I know your family. I know your story. I know what God is doing in you and now I want to **tell you who you are becoming**. Not a kid filled with fear, but a leader filled with more power and love and discipline to get things done than you probably realize.

That's the great thing about a coach or a mentor. **They have the power to remind us who we are, even when we aren't sure.** And that wasn't the only way Paul coached Timothy. Paul gave Timothy advice on everything from how to fix his stomach problems (1 Timothy 5:23), how to use the Scriptures (2 Timothy 3:16-17), how to handle money (1 Timothy 6), and how to impress older people (1 Timothy 4:12-13).

In other words, Paul wasn't just Timothy's Bible teacher or pastor. Paul was able to guide Timothy in every area of life because Paul had experience Timothy didn't. And that's true for *all* of us. There are people who are farther along and can speak wisdom into areas of our lives where we might not even know we need it. The key is being self-aware enough to know we need guidance from others, and then making it happen.

What's one area of life where you could use a little advice from somebody who has been where you are now?

....

....

....

Maybe you need a mentor who . . . .

- specializes in the career field you want.

- has been to the school you're attending.

- knows your family and can give you advice.

- has lived with roommates.

- has commuted to school before.

- has managed a long-distance dating relationship.

- has survived a breakup before.

In reality, you probably won't find all the expertise you need in one person, and that's okay. When it comes to mentors,

you need a team.

You need a group of people, a little farther down the road, who can tell you what is up ahead, what to watch out for, and how to get from where you are now to where you want to go.

Some coaches or mentors, like Paul, will be a part of your life for the long haul. But for others, it may just be for a season. Either way, anytime you're in a new season, getting a coaching team in place is a great idea.

In the space below, brainstorm some characteristics that might be helpful for you in a coach or a mentor.

....

....

....

Chances are, as you were thinking about it, a few people came to mind. Go ahead and write the names of potential coaches or mentors that might be good to have on your team this year.

Who COULD be on my team this year?

....

....

....

....

You need
a team.

We (Gerald and Crystal) are so convinced that having a team of mentors is a game changer for you, that we've created a system so you don't even have to tell the coaches or mentors in your life what you want them to do. You send one text and we do the rest.

If you're ready to make a team for this semester, turn the page and get started.

ON MY
TEAM.ORG

Until now, you've probably been *assigned* coaches, teachers, counselors, and youth pastors. That was great, but things are changing. **Now, as an adult, you get to choose the people on your team**. And who you choose may be one of the most important adult decisions you make. So how do you choose?

Well, first, let's assume your parents are still acting as advisors in your life. They may not be telling you when to wake up, what time to come home or remind you to eat more veggies, but chances are they still know you better than anyone else and still want the best for you. So let's keep them on the list.

Who else?

- As you think of everyone you know, **start with people who are little farther along in life than you.** You probably already have great friends who are figuring out the after-graduation life together. Keep them! But for your coaching team, you'll want three to five people who have already been there. People who can help you see what you don't see and help you through what they've already been through.

- **Make wise decisions in their own life.** This is a no-brainer, right? If someone makes bad decisions in their own life, they shouldn't help make decisions for yours. You can still be friends with them, of course. But they're not on your team. That's just a bad idea.

- **Care about you enough to tell you what you don't want to hear.** We all have those people who will tell us what we want to hear and make us feel good about our own ideas. But if you want to make consistently *wise* decisions, you're going to need somebody who loves you enough to disagree with you, to point out when your plans don't set you up for the best outcomes, and to help you figure out a better alternative.

So that's it: farther along than you, wise in their own life, and cares about you. Do a few people you look up to fit that criteria? Good. Write their names here.

....

....

....

....

....

Now, it's time to make the ask.

We know that asking anyone for a favor can be a little scary, but trust us. Asking someone to be on your team will make their day. And it doesn't have to be complicated. **We wrote the text for you!** You can type it out yourself or just take a picture of the message on the next page and text it to them.

No matter how you ask, make sure your mentor goes to **OnMyTeam.org** to sign up to be on your team.

Hey. You may know that I recently graduated. As I move toward what's next, I realize that I'm going to need some wisdom and encouragement from people a little farther down the road than me.

.In other words, **I need a team.**

I need a few trusted adults who make wise decisions in their own life and care about mine that will check in occasionally and help me navigate the first few months of adult life. Would you consider being on my team between now and the end of the semester? Sign up is easy. Just go to **www.OnMyTeam.org** and click "I'm a mentor". You'll get emails letting you know when to check in, what to talk about with me, and why all this matters. If you can't, don't worry! Life is really busy and I get that. Just let me know by shooting a text that says
"Hey. I can't be on your team this semester, but I'll be praying for you and cheering from the sidelines."
Thanks again for being the kind of adult students like me want on their team!

WHEN IT
COMES TO MY
COMMUNITY

STARTING NOW
I WILL . . .

....
....
....
....
....
....
....
....
....
....
....
....
....
....
....

IDENTITY

WEEK 02

identity

[ahy-**den**-ti-tee, ih-**den**-]

Definition: If you're reading this, you have one.

Definition: The thing you try to hide when you find out the hard way why there's a "no cooking in the dorm" policy. (Who knew grilling paninis with a clothing iron was such a fire hazard?)

Definition: The part of you that's wildly different from who you were in middle school . . . yet somehow still the same.

Definition: Something you feel like you should know about yourself but you're still trying to figure out.

Definition: Something other people have always had an opinion about, but you get to decide for yourself . . . starting now.

If someone you grew up with were to describe you, what do you think they'd say? Maybe all your life you've been known for being the comedian among your friends or for being really weirdly good at math. Or maybe you were known as the exact opposite—the kid who always struggled in school, or was picked last for dodge ball.

Good or bad, what are a few things you're known for?

....

....

....

We're all known for something. Which is why this new phase of life can be weird or jolting. Because if you've moved to a different town, you've probably already noticed no one knows (or cares) what you were known for in high school. You were the valedictorian? No one knows that. You were known for a few mistakes? No one knows that either. You were funny, popular or nerdy? No. One. Knows. Even if you didn't move away, graduating high school probably means you have new classes, a new job, a different schedule. And in the same way, you're interacting with a different circle of people, some of them new, who may not think of you as who you've always been. It's a fresh start. Which can be freeing . . . but also terrifying.

And all of it can make you feel like you don't know yourself. Do you really like basketball? Or did you just play because that's what you were known for? Are you really *that* into theatre? Or, was it something you just sort of fell into because that's where your friends were? Sometime in the next few weeks, or during the course of this semester, you may find yourself wondering who you really are and who you're supposed to be, *starting now*. When that happens, it can be helpful to know you aren't the first to wonder. On day three of last week, we looked at part of what King David wrote in Psalm 139. Let's go back to the start of the psalm and see how he begins.

> *You have searched me, Lord,*
> *and you know me. You know when I sit and when I*
> *rise; you perceive my thoughts from afar.*
> *You discern my going out and my lying down;*
> *you are familiar with all my ways.*
> *Before a word is on my tongue*
> *you, Lord, know it completely.*
> *You hem me in behind and before,*
> *and you lay your hand upon me.*
> *Such knowledge is too wonderful for me,*
> *too lofty for me to attain.*
> *(Psalm 139:1-6 NIV)*

The truth is, like David experienced, your Heavenly Father knows you. He knows you better than you know yourself— the you, who you used to be, and the you, you are going to become. He knows the words you want to say before you say them, the thoughts you think late at night, the parts of you that aren't just outward facing, but inward as well.

It's almost as if David is saying, you are more known than you sometimes feel. Which is great news, especially when starting something new. Just because no one knows you yet, doesn't mean you aren't known. Because **who you are is more than what you're known for** or what people think of you. Your Heavenly Father knows you, the *real* you, better than anyone. While a lot of life is changing, that part isn't. Your identity and what God thinks about you didn't move one bit when you started college because . . .

where you are doesn't change who you are.

What are some things God knows about you that others may not?

....

....

....

What words do you think God would use to describe you?

....

....

....

Now, take a look at how David continues this Psalm in verse 14.

I praise you because I am fearfully and wonderfully made; your works are wonderful, I know that full well.
(Psalm 139:14 NIV)

What would change for you if you walked into every new situation this year knowing "full well" that you are fearfully and wonderfully made? How might that change . . .

how you feel?

....

....

how you act?

....

....

how you speak?

....

....

The truth is, **what you are known for may change this year.** What people think of you or know about you may change in these months of new places and new relationships and new status. Or it may stay the same. But what you are known for, from the past, or in your new present, is not WHO you are. **Who you are is *fearfully* and *wonderfully* made in the image of God.** And the One who made you is the only One who gets the final word on who you are. Let that be what keeps you steady. When nothing else feels stable, when everything around you feels like it is changing, who you are does not change not when your identity comes from the one who created you in the first place. You were made in the image of God and **where you are doesn't change who you are.**

Where
you are
doesn't
change
who
you are.

DAY**2**

One of the BEST parts of starting college is the independence that comes with it. You get to decide all kinds of things that used to be decided *for* you.

List 5 things you get to decide now that you've never had to decide before

1. ....

2. ....

3. ....

4. ....

5. ....

In some ways, that sounds great. But maybe you've noticed that even though you technically have more independence than you ever have before, there are probably areas that you don't feel as much control over as you had imagined. Maybe you got stuck with a roommate, and you wish you could change it but you can't. Maybe you got stuck with an 8am class. And while pretty much everyone else is sleeping in, you're hoofing it in the cold to listen to a lecture. Or maybe you feel stuck, but in different ways. Maybe you feel stuck with . . .

- your academic ability.

- your family's finances.

- your dating life (or lack thereof).

- your personality.

- your past.

We all know what it feels like to be stuck in a situation, like you don't have any power. In reality, it feels like your life story (at least in that area), is already written for you.

What's one area of life where you feel like you can't change your situation or your story?

....

....

....

Sometimes we feel stuck in a life story and don't even realize it. Maybe you've never thought about it but . . .

- people from your town never really leave for good.

- people from your family don't go to college or don't graduate.

- people with *your* past always seem to go back to *their* past.

- people with your abilities always seem to pick this major or that one.

- people like you don't do .... or always do ....

And in some ways, it can feel like your story is already written. That's what's tricky about college. We're told the possibilities are endless, that we can do anything or become anyone. And that's true! But without realizing it, sometimes we stop believing that. Or we begin thinking that's true for *most* people, just not us. We start telling ourselves, "this is just how it is" or "this is just who I am" . And suddenly, we're in a new place, but stuck in the same old life story.

And, *that* has been happening since the beginning. The book of Isaiah is known as a book of prophecy. Prophecy of what? Well, the chapter we are looking at is thought to have been written when the Israelites were in exile in Babylon. Exile just means they had been taken from their land and moved to a foreign land with foreign rulers and foreign gods. Things were not exactly looking up. Whatever good life they had before is long gone. Whatever hope they have for the future is miniscule, at best. Sure, they were in a new land, but this wasn't a land full of hope and promise. They were in a place that constantly reminded them of the sad story they were living.

And then Isaiah comes along, and the words God speaks through him, to a group of people convinced they were stuck in one particular kind of story was nothing short of incredible.

> *"Forget the former things, do not dwell on the past.*
> *See, I am doing a new thing! Now it springs up;*
> *do you not perceive it? I am making a way in the*
> *wilderness and streams in the wasteland."*
> *(Isaiah 43:18-19 NIV)*

Can you imagine what a message like this would have felt like to people stuck in a strange land, stuck in a pattern of defeat, stuck in a way of thinking that would have felt permanent and never ending? A message like this was a game changer. Why?

Because it suggested **there was something happening they couldn't imagine or plan for or see yet.** God wasn't telling them to get used to their old ways, but that He was making a new way. Think about the word-picture Isaiah is writing here. If you've ever been to the wilderness, there aren't usually paved paths with signage. And, if you've ever been to a desert (translated here as wasteland), there are *no* streams. That's what makes it a desert. God is basically saying, "You can't see the way out yet, because it's not there yet. Even if it seems impossible right now, I'm carving a *new* path for you, one you can't imagine yet."

And maybe that's exactly what you need to hear.
Because in this new phase you are surrounded by new friends and new classes and a new apartment and new independence—more than you've ever experienced before, but *your* life story still feels like there are only a few paths it can take. Because of your past, or your family, or your finances or your patterns, it feels like many of your decisions are already made for you. It may have never occurred to you that you can decide to go a new way. In fact, **maybe you've been working so hard at choosing from the paths you already see, it hasn't occurred to you that there are other possibilities at all.**

If that's you, the message from the book of Isaiah may just be what you need to hear because it's a reminder that God does not get stuck. God is not limited by the past. God does new things. He makes a way in the wilderness and creates streams in the desert.* **Your past doesn't get to decide who you get to be.** Your old story doesn't have to be your current story.

Decide now to decide for yourself

who you will be and what you will do. God isn't holding your old story against you. And you shouldn't either. For Him, the possibilities are endless. And as His child, He can make anything possible for you. Choose to believe God is a God

---

* In exile, the Israelites couldn't have imagined life or the story of their people ever being any different. But God's definition of "new" goes beyond what we imagine. In fact, many believe the "new thing" God was referring to here wasn't just rescue from exile or their current circumstances, but rescue for the entire story of humanity through Jesus.

who always rescues people who are stuck and creates a way forward. *Starting now.*

What are some ways you tend to assume your past (family, town, friends, decisions) has already decided your future?

....

....

....

Where do you need something new to happen in your life? (Circle what applies to you)

> In toxic friendships.

> In unhealthy dating relationships.

> In the way you view yourself.

> In a lingering reputation.

> In the possibilities (or lack of possibilities) you believe for your future.

What would you do differently if you decided now to decide for yourself what your life will become?

....

....

....

What could you miss out on if you continue in the same life patterns as if your life was already decided for you?

....

....

....

Take a few minutes to pray and ask God to help you see where you have begun to believe your life is already decided. Ask for His help in seeing a new direction He wants you to go in and ask for the courage to take the first step.

Decide now
to decide
yourself.

DAY3

Have you ever heard something everyone seems to agree with, but you find yourself wondering, "is that even true?!"

Like, kangaroos can't jump backwards.

Or alpacas can die of loneliness.

Or Dalmatians are born without any spots.

At some point or another, we've probably all felt that way about something in the Bible. It sounds interesting, but is it really *true*? It seems like we're *supposed* to agree, like everyone else agrees, but at first glance it just isn't that . . . believable.

There's a verse written by Jesus' brother, James,* that's one of those things that doesn't quite seem believable when you first read it. James writes:

> *Consider it pure joy, my brothers and sisters,*
> *whenever you face trials of many kinds.*
> *(James 1:2 NIV)*

---

*Did you catch that? He was Jesus' brother! Don't skip over how amazing that is. Can you imagine growing up with Jesus in your family? You would never win an argument! The interesting thing is, it took James a long time to believe that his brother was actually the Son of God. In fact, he spent his whole life before Jesus died not believing his brother was who he said he was. It wasn't until after the resurrection that James saw his brother as his Lord and Savior.

James uses the word "trials" here, which is another way of saying, troubles or ordeals, or hardships. Basically James is saying the most challenging things in your life? Consider those things *joy*. Is he crazy? It was like the 1st century equivalent of being told, every cloud has a silver lining! Or, no pain, no gain! Obviously if James had ever experienced . . .

> an 8am class,

> food served in a school dining hall,

> getting cut from a sports team,

> a roommate who leaves their stuff everywhere and has no consideration for you,

> an essay on the complicated life of plankton,

he'd think differently.

But the thing is, James *did* know hardship and the people he was writing to knew them as well. His letter was written to Jewish people across the world who had decided to follow Jesus and at the time, very few things would put you in more danger than being Jewish + a Jesus follower. So much danger your life could be on the line. And in light of all that, James says, "Consider it pure joy"?! Of course it sounds unbelievable. Because it is for most of us. Our thought process looks like this:

Trouble = Difficult. And Difficult = Bad.

We don't often think:

Trouble = Difficult. And Difficult = Joy!

Thankfully James goes on to give us some insight into why he says what he does, explaining why he would say something so counterintuitive:

. . . because you know that the testing of your faith produces perseverance. Let perseverance finish its work so that you may be mature and complete, not lacking anything.
(James 1:3-4 NIV)

James isn't saying we should enjoy trouble just for trouble's sake, or that we should like our challenges because they're fun. No, James recognizes that there's a potential benefit when we run into difficult or challenging situations. *There's an opportunity.* Troubles can make us miserable or troubles can make us better. And they make us better not just when we get through them to the other side. They make us better, because when we let them, they produce something in us. To use James's words, difficulties produce:

Perseverance:
the ability to keep going even when you want to give up.

Maturity:
wisdom into our circumstances and relationships you might not otherwise have.

Completeness:
a sense of wholeness for having been through something difficult and coming out the other side with a better sense of who you are as a result.

In other words, James is saying what you do, and what you work through, affects *who* you become, one way or the other. Every time you face a challenge, **every time you do something difficult you have an opportunity to become the kind of person who can do difficult things**. You become a person of character who isn't afraid of tough challenges. On the flip side, every time you distract or delay or avoid, you miss out on a chance to grow into the kind of person who can do difficult things.

What's one difficult thing you've gone through that helped you grow?

....

....

What could you potentially miss out on if you fail to develop perseverance and endurance in this stage of life?

....

....

What's something you've been avoiding because it seems challenging or difficult?

....

....

One of the best things about starting a new phase of life is you get to decide what kind of person you want to be, *starting now*. And while you can be an avoider, a delayer, or a distracter when it comes to difficult things (most of us are), one of the best decisions you can make is to:

be the kind of person who does something difficult.

Because, as challenging as starting college may be, it won't be the last challenging thing you do in life. In fact, chances are there are some really good parts of life ahead that are also going to be really *hard*. So develop the strength, the grit, and the perseverance *now* that you'll need *then*.

What's the first thing you would do if you decided to "count it all joy" and dive head first into something difficult you've been avoiding?

Be the kind
of person
who does
something
difficult.

Is there anything better than watching epic fail videos on the internet? We don't care who you are, those will never *not* be funny. Set a timer for three minutes and go watch a few. Just make sure when the timer goes off that you actually come back to this, okay?

Welcome back.

You know what makes those videos so great? *That we've all been there.* Chances are you know what it's like to slam into a glass door or trip up the stairs, but once it's over, we can usually laugh it off (or post video of it). Because embarrassment on a small scale is easy to recover from.

But we also know that not all failure is funny. In fact, maybe the idea of failing in some areas fills you with anxiety and dread. And for good reason. Maybe you worry about failing academically and letting yourself down or letting your parents down. Maybe you worry about failing financially as you carry the weight of student loans and having to buy your own groceries now. Or maybe you're scared about failing God, about making big promises to Him, but not being able to keep them.

The options are endless. But no matter what area of life you are fearing failure, here is one uncomfortable truth:

Failure is inevitable.

It's going to happen. No matter how good your intentions are or how hard you try, at some point you are going to fail. (Aren't you glad you decided to sit down and read this today?) But before you throw your hands up and quit *everything*, stick with us for a minute.

Failure isn't unique to you. Actually, the Apostle Paul* understood failure all too well. And he wrote . . .

> *I do not understand what I do. For what I*
> *want to do I do not do, but what I hate I do.*
> *(Romans 7:15 NIV)*

(If we're being honest, we think we could agree some days that line hits more close to home than we'd like.) Paul goes on to explain what he means a few verses later. Maybe you can relate.

> *For I know that good itself does not dwell in me,*
> *that is, in my sinful nature. For I have the desire to*
> *do what is good, but I cannot carry it out. For I*
> *do not do the good I want to do, but the evil I*
> *do not want to do—this I keep on doing.*
> *(Romans 7:18-19 NIV)*

If the guy responsible for the spread of Christianity outside of Israel sometimes felt like a failure, than we're in good company. Paul understood that because of the nature of the world we live in and the nature of us as human beings, failure would be part of us. We'll never outgrow it. So, the question is . . .

---

* Chances are you've heard of the Apostle Paul. He is the one responsible for the spread of Christianity outside of Jerusalem and the Mediterranean rim. In fact, while Jesus' original 12 disciples had heard Jesus say directly to them that they were to take his message of love and forgiveness to the larger world, they tended to stick close to home. Paul was different. Paul saw his mission as being to the Gentiles— those were people who weren't Jewish. You could say that if it weren't for Paul, you and I would have never heard about Jesus. Christianity would have stayed a predominately Jewish religion centered in the Middle East.

what happens next?

People respond to failure in different ways. Some of us run from it. Some of us brush it off like it's no big deal. Some of us are paralyzed by it. But we all face the same danger when we bump into the inevitable failure: the temptation to feel terrible about ourselves. Meaning, when we fail, it's easy to begin to think we ourselves are the failure. We take something we did and make it something we are.

Sometimes we even assume God sees us that way.

Here's the truth about this new phase of life you've just entered. You will mess up. You will fail. After all, you're new at this whole adult thing.

The question isn't whether you will make some poor choices. The question is what will you do when you do? Will you see your failure as something you *did* or something you *are*?

Paul goes on in his letter to the Romans and says this:

> *For those who are led by the Spirit of God are
> the children of God. The Spirit you received does
> not make you slaves, so that you live in fear again;
> rather, the Spirit you received brought about your
> adoption to sonship. And by him we cry,
> "Abba, Father." The Spirit himself testified with
> our spirit that we are God's children.*
> (Romans 8:14-16 NIV)

Did you catch what Paul referred to four times in those three verses? *We are God's children.* We aren't our failures. We are adopted into God's family. Once you are in, *you are in.* No failure, big or small changes our standing with God.

Of course that doesn't mean when we do fail that we avoid consequences. Being in God's family is not a free pass from the effects of failures, but it is a reminder that WHO we are does not change because of what we've done. What God has said it true of us, *remains* true of us.

In other words,

failing does not make you a failure.

What are some things you typically say to yourself when you mess up?

....

....

....

What would you say differently if you believed failing was something you did, not something you are?

....

....

....

Are there any previous failures you need to stop let defining how you think about you?

....

....

Spend a few minutes thanking God for His grace over your failures—both past and future.

Failing
does not
make you
a failure.

DAY 5

Let's talk about your sex life.

Well, that got awkward fast, didn't it?

Don't worry. You're not going to get "the talk". (Hopefully somebody, somewhere has already taken care of that.) But as you begin this phase of life, sex, and specifically *your* sex life, is something important to think about. And let's be honest. Chances are you're already thinking about it. It'd be impossible to *not* think about something that shows up in . . .

- Netflix shows.

- music.

- commercials.

- social media.

- basically the entire internet.

- maybe even some of your professors' lectures.

Sex is everywhere in our world, and along with it are messages about what is okay/not okay, what is normal, what is off-limits, and what is just fine. Take a moment and think about those messages.

What are some messages the average person your age gets about sex every day?

....

....

Maybe the idea of thinking about God and sex seems a little strange. But the truth is, God very much cares about your sex life, and chances are, you have an idea of what He has to say about it. Think back on the messages you've heard about sex coming from the Church or other Christians.

Based on the messages you've heard, what do you think God's plan is for sex?

....

....

The ideas of sex and marriage vary in different cultures. And the culture when Jesus was alive had an idea of what was okay and what wasn't, which is why, when giving His most famous sermon of all time, Jesus used the phrase, *"You have heard it said."* That was His way of saying, there was an expectation for the time and everyone knew it. So He goes on:

> *"You have heard that it was said,*
> *'You shall not commit adultery.'"*
> *(Matthew 5:27 NIV)*

This was a throw back to the Ten Commandments—the set of laws Jewish people would have been very familiar with. And commandment #7 was as clear as it could be: "You shall *not* commit adultery." The Jewish cultural message about sex boiled down to this: don't have sex with somebody else's husband or wife.

Sounds like a reasonable rule. Hard to argue with. But then Jesus adds something that *wasn't* part of the cultural norm.

"You have heard that it was said, 'You shall not commit adultery.' **But I tell you that anyone who looks at a woman lustfully has already committed adultery with her in his heart.**"
(Matthew 5:27-28 NIV emphasis added)

So what is Jesus doing here? He doesn't throw out the old definition of adultery. Instead, He expands on it. The Jewish people had always believed "the line" they should not cross was having sex with someone's spouse. Jesus agreed but basically said, "sex is more than you think it is." Not only does Jesus' definition of sex include what we do physically but, according to Him, it also includes how we think about another person, how we look at another person, *and* how we treat them.

Maybe that's surprising to you because you thought all God cared about was whether you were a virgin or not. So you thought everything other than crossing "that line" was okay. Or maybe you felt like because you've already had sex, honoring God was impossible. Either way, Jesus is saying when we think sex is only about one thing, and that one thing is all God cares about, we're missing the point. **Sex was always supposed to be about more than just one act, just your body, or even just you.**

So what does this mean for you? It means your sex life, the sex life God wants for you is about more than just one thing. It includes . . .

- how you see people.

- how you think about people.

- the value you give other people.

- the way you treat other people.

In other words, **when it comes to sex, God isn't just interested in what you're doing but who you're becoming.** That's why Jesus brings up *the heart* in His sermon on the side of the mountain. Because He wanted us to know that what He wants for us is about more than just what we do. It's about what we think, what we feel, and who we are. So, are you becoming the kind of person who . . .

- is trustworthy?
- is kind?
- honors God and others?
- puts others first?
- protects others' futures?

All of those things add up to being a person of *integrity*. And just like you can be a person of integrity in your academics, your friendships, and your finances, you can (and should, no matter what your past experiences) have integrity in your sex life. Sexual integrity is about more than just saving sex until marriage or feeling guilty for *not* waiting. It's choosing to honor in how you think about, treat, and value the people you date *starting now*.

What are some things someone who chooses to live with sexual integrity might do?

....

....

....

Integrity matters. Sure, it matters to God, but it also matters to you. Think about it. Chances are when you think of the person you want to date or even marry, you think of someone with all of those characteristics. Someone trustworthy, kind, honorable, selfless. You want to date someone with integrity in every area of their life. So if you want these things in someone else, why not work on being those things too?

Become the kind of person you want to be with.

Think about the kind of person you want to be with, not just who you want to take to a fraternity formal but the kind of person you want to be with long-term, the kind of person you want to end up with.

What are some words that describe them?

....

....

....

What is your dream man/woman like when it comes to . . .

how they treat their friends?

....

....

how they treat people they date?

....

....

how they treat their families?

....

....

how they see themselves?

....

....

how they think/talk about the opposite sex?

....

....

the kind of sexual content they allow themselves to watch/listen to?

....

....

If these are ideals for the person you want to be with, where are the areas you may need to do some work in your own life?

....

....

....

Pray and ask for God's help in becoming the kind of person you want to be with in each of those areas.

Become
the kind of
person you
want to
be with.

VISION
BOARD

Starting now, you get to decide what kind of person you want to be. But deciding to be something and actually BEING that thing are . . . well . . . different. We all tend to drift off course, make decisions we regret, or be influenced to act like someone we don't recognize. And often it's not that we *decided* to change. It's simply because we forget.

That's why one of the best things you can do for you as you're getting started in this new stage of life is to create a visual reminder of who you want to be.

Before you get started, flip through the first two weeks of this journal and jot down a list of words or phrases that stuck out to you.

Use those as a starting point to brainstorm a list of ideas that could remind you of the decisions you've made and the person you want to become.

....

....

....

....

When you have a list, you're going to make a visual reminder of who you want to be, starting now. There are a few ways you can do this.

Option 1:
Grab some old magazines and newspapers. Cut out photos or phrases that remind you of your decisions and either pin them to a bulletin board or paste them onto a posterboard to hang in your room.

Option 2:
For each word or phrase you listed above, do an image search on Google or on Pinterest. Collect the images and phrases onto a single page and print it to hang on your wall.

No matter how you make your reminder board, the point is to have a visual cue of who YOU want to be, starting now.

WHEN IT COMES TO MY IDENTITY

STARTING NOW
I WILL . . .

FAITH

WEEK 03

faith

[feyth]

Definition: The thing you need to have if you want tonight to be fresh curly fries night in the dining hall.

Definition: A belief or beliefs you may have picked up from your mom, your grandpa or the really attractive person who invited you to youth group in high school.

Definition: A state in which you have a *lot* of questions . . . but also aren't sure if it's okay to ask them.

Definition: The thing that people tell you will go away in college but that's not exactly what you want to happen.

Definition: Something every person must question, investigate, and reimagine for themselves—including you . . . starting now.

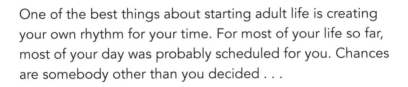

One of the best things about starting adult life is creating your own rhythm for your time. For most of your life so far, most of your day was probably scheduled for you. Chances are somebody other than you decided . . .

- when your first class started.

- how many classes you had to take.

- when you could eat lunch.

- what time you had practice.

- when you had a curfew.

But now? So much is up to you! Hate early classes? Don't sign up for them. Prefer a Monday, Wednesday, Friday schedule? You can make that happen. Study all night and sleep all day? Your choice. Get up at dawn and eat dinner with all the senior citizens? You can do that, too. The point is, your rhythm and how you live is up to you.

The same is true with your relationship with God. *You* get to decide what your walk with God looks like. No one decides it for you! Look at what the Apostle Paul wrote in a letter to the Christians living in Phillipi about this idea.

*Therefore, my dear friends, as you have always obeyed—not only in my presence, but now much more in my absence—**continue to work out your salvation** with fear and trembling, for it is God who works in you to will and to act in order to fulfill his good purpose. (Philippians 2:12-13 NIV emphasis added)**

Notice, Paul doesn't tell the Christians in Philippi to . . .

- go to church more.

- pray more.

- read the Bible more.

- give more.

- serve more.

He tells them to "work out your salvation". Not work *for* your salvation. (This isn't about doing things to be right with God or get into Heaven.) Paul is talking to people who *already* follow Jesus. So he's saying, because you're already right with God, you need to live accordingly—not by following a formula, but by investing in a relationship—a relationship that is as unique as you are. Should you pray? Sure, but when and how often is up to you. Should you read the Bible? Absolutely, but how you read is your call. Should we do all the things that help us grow closer to God? Yes, but the rhythm and the speed and the pace of it is something we have to work out for ourselves. In other words, to have a mature faith, you have to . . .

work out your walk with God.

---

*Remember, being a follower of Jesus in the 1st century was dangerous. Much of Paul's life spent sharing Jesus with others was done knowing at any point he could be arrested (he was), jailed (he was), hunted (he was) and even killed (he ultimately died because of his faith). So you can imagine the urgency as he writes to these new churches with. Every letter is written knowing he may not make it back to see them again. So what are the most important/valuable lessons he could leave them with?

Take a look at the list below. Circle the things that are already a regular part of your walk with God and underline ones you would like to begin or experience more often.

Bible reading

Bible memorizing

Devotionals

Prayer

Worship

Rest

Accountability

Serving

Giving

Attending church

Attending small group Bible study or discipleship

Take some time to think about the way these things have already been incorporated into your life and ask yourself if they're working well. If not, what can you begin to do to work out your walk with God in a way that best fits *your* life?

....

....

....

It's tempting to look at other people and think we should connect with God the same way they do. But like any relationship, your relationship with God is unique to you. You'll have your own rhythm, traditions, and habits. Just like God made you unique, how you connect with Him best is unique to you.

Back to Paul. In the rest of the verse he reminds the Philippians to work out their walk with God *"with fear and trembling for it is God who works in you to will and to act in order to fulfill his good purpose"*. Paul is reminding them that God is at work in them. Think about that. The same God who made mountains and volcanoes and galaxies and solar systems desires to be at work in their—*and your*—hearts. And that's a big deal.

Spending time with God, maturing in your faith isn't like picking your class schedule or managing your study habits. It's way bigger than that. The same infinite, mesmerizing, omnipotent Being that spoke all creation into existence now wants to speak into your heart, into your life on a *regular* basis, to help you work at becoming the best version of you, you could possible be. And He has given you the freedom to decide the details of how, when, and how often.

Imagine that for a second.

What are a few areas where you could use God's guidance right now?

....

....

....

What are a few areas where you could use His power or His comfort?

....

....

....

How could this semester be different for you if you decided to connect with Him regularly in a meaningful way?

....

....

....

There are a lot of ways to connect with God, but here are four big ones that are a great place to start.

1. HEAR from God

Maybe you read ten chapters of the Bibile at a time. Maybe you're a memorizer. Maybe you're a meditator. Maybe you're an audio-Bible listener. No matter what it is, work out how you will hear from God this semester.

How do I hear from God best?

....

....

....

How will I hear from God regularly this semester?

....

....

....

2. PRAY to God

Talking is a big part of any relationship. So is listening. But in a world with a lot of noise, finding the time and space to pray also takes intentionality.

Where and when can I pray daily?

....

....

....

How will I remind myself to pray to God regularly this semester?

....

....

....

3. TALK about God

Just like talking TO God matters, talking ABOUT Him with others can encourage, challenge, and sharpen your faith like nothing else. Maybe for you that happens with a small group, a Bible study, or a mentor.

Who can I talk to honestly and often about my relationship with God?

....

....

....

How will I schedule my life so these conversations happen regularly?

....

....

....

4. LIVE for God

Spending time with God is only one way we know Him. We also get to know Him by living out our faith and seeing Him work through us. One of the best ways to do that is serving others regularly.

What are some ways God can use me to serve others this semester?

....

....

....

How will I schedule serving so that it isn't random but something that happens regularly?

....

....

....

Work out
your walk
with God.

Starting college can feel like one big growth spurt. Maybe you're not growing taller anymore (one can still dream, right?) but all of the sudden you're stretching and growing in . . .

- academics.

- study habits.

- maturity.

- social skills.

- financial management.

- time management.

- and about a million other areas.

What's one area of life where you have noticed yourself growing or changing recently?

....

....

....

For a lot of these areas, you are growing out of necessity. You have to learn how to manage finances and time and study habits. But when it comes to growing in your faith in this new life stage it can actually be a bit more complicated, because it doesn't always happen naturally. Not only that, what does growth in faith even look like? Or, how does someone grow in spiritual maturity?

The author of Hebrews* tackled that very subject with a little analogy.

> *In fact, though by this time you ought to be teachers, you need someone to teach you the elementary truths of God's word all over again. You need milk, not solid food! Anyone who lives on milk, being still an infant, is not acquainted with the teaching about righteousness. But solid food is for the mature, who by constant use have trained themselves to distinguish good from evil.*
> *(Hebrews 5:12-14 NIV)*

The author notices the lack of spiritual growth or maturity among the Jewish believers and uses the analogy of children moving from milk to solid food. People often use this analogy now to talk about the way people teach or study Scripture. They say the key to spiritual growth is deeper or more mature teaching or Bible study. Basically, the idea is . . .

Milk is for babies.
Spiritual "milk" is like baby food. It's simple. Uncomplicated. Easy to digest.

Solid food is for the mature.
Spiritual "solid food"** is information that is more complicated, more sophisticated, and more difficult to understand.

---

*Because Hebrews is a letter written to Jewish people who had decided to follow Jesus, the entire book is filled with comparisons of Jesus being made to a great high priest and other Jewish language/terminology. This can make it harder for us to understand the context, but would have made it very effective for the people it was originally written for.

**Or "meat" in some translations

We tend to think of it this way:

Immature faith = simple Bible knowledge

Mature faith = complicated or advanced Bible knowledge

It's not a bad analogy, but here's the problem: the audience—Jewish believers—were already familiar with the Scriptures. As children, they (at least the boys) were trained to memorize long passages and sit in teachings at the synagogue. This was not an uneducated or unstudied audience. Needing to *study* more information wasn't really what was keeping these believers from growing in their faith. Take a second look at how the author describes maturity in verse 14:

Solid food is for the mature. Who by . . .
Constant use **(action)**
Have trained themselves **(action)**
To distinguish the difference in right and wrong.
(decision that leads to action)

It seems the author isn't just concerned with the amount or the kind of information the Hebrews are learning, but also what they are *doing* with it.

Another ancient writer to Jewish believers, James,* puts it this way:

> *Do not merely listen to the word, and*
> *so deceive yourselves. Do what it says.*
> *(James 1:22 NIV)*

In other words, it can be really easy to convince ourselves that the more complicated the teaching we hear, or the longer the message we hear, or the more time spent reading the Bible, the more mature we are. But James and the author

---

*Jesus' brother, James, wrote a letter to Jews scattered in other regions. He also would have grown up in a Jewish context, knowing all the right stuff taught in Scripture.

of Hebrews are saying that's just the start. Real growth, real maturity, real faith is in what we DO with what we've heard or read. That's how we go deeper in our Christian walk. That's how we grow. That's how we become who God has created us to become—not by accident, but by action.

What are some things the Bible teaches that are easy for you to put into practice?

....

....

....

What are some things that you *know* but have a difficult time doing?

....

....

....

In your opinion, which is easier (circle one) . . .

Learning what God says   **Doing what God says**

Just like your knowledge of everything else is expanding in college, your understanding of the story of God should expand as well. Information only leads to maturity when we put it into practice. In other words,

when it comes to your faith, deeper is about doing—not just knowing.

Pray and ask God to reveal areas where you need to put your faith into practice. As He brings answers to mind, write them below.

....

....

....

....

....

When it comes to your faith, deeper is about doing— not just knowing.

Most of us live with a lot of unspoken rules. We don't talk about them because everyone already knows them.

They're rules like:

- Don't eat your roommate's food.

- It's not okay to "borrow" a toothbrush.

- You should never pee in the shower.
  (You knew that, right?)

On top of those, and about a thousand other unspoken social agreements, we also know there are some subjects that are okay to talk about and others that are *not* okay. Of course we all have that *one* friend who has no clue about these social rules, but for the most part we all agree that some subjects, some ideas, and some thoughts are ones *we just don't talk about.*

If you grew up in church or around Christians, one of those off-limits subjects for you was probably *doubt.* The idea of saying things out loud that seemed hard to believe or at least a little awkward, was a big "no". But let's be honest, there can be a lot of questions when it comes to faith.

Think about it. We spend a lot of time talking about . . .

- a God we can't see.

- a flood that covers the whole Earth.

- seas that part.

- blind people becoming not blind.

- sick people becoming not sick.

- one Guy who DIED and came back to life.

And nobody has questions about this? *Really?*

The truth is you probably do have questions and maybe some doubts about the whole thing. All of us do at some point or another. We just don't talk about them often. For a lot of us, we don't even want to think about them. And even if we talk about doubt in theory, like "everybody doubts", most of us don't spend a lot of time thinking through our own personal doubts.

In your opinion, why is it so difficult to talk about our doubts?

....

....

....

So why do we keep our doubts to ourselves? *Because saying them out loud is scary.* When faith is such a big part of your life, a part of your friendships or family, or how you date or make decisions, voicing what you doubt feels like it could make the whole structure of your life fall apart.

That's why sometimes we just choose NOT to ask questions. When the thought creeps in our mind "what if this *isn't* true?" we try to put it out of our minds or think about something else.

But maybe you've discovered **not dealing with your doubts doesn't make them go away.** Sure, they may be quiet for a minute. They may not bug you for a day or two. But eventually, they always come back, sometimes louder than before, more nagging and insistent than ever.

So then, **what do you do with your doubt?**

First? We acknowledge it. Yes, you read that right. *Accept your doubt,* that it exists and that your doubt isn't unique to you. All throughout the documents of the Old and New Testament, we find stories of people who had questions— good ones. People who wrestled with doubt. One of our favorite examples of this comes from an expert in Jewish law, named Nicodemus.*

Like a lot of us who are religious, it was probably awkward for Nicodemus to admit he had some questions. But he asks them anyway.

> **"How can someone be born when they are old?"**
> Nicodemus asked. *"Surely they cannot enter a second time into their mother's womb to be born!"*
> Jesus answered, *"Very truly I tell you, no one can enter the kingdom of God unless they are born of water and the Spirit. Flesh gives birth to flesh, but the Spirit gives birth to spirit.*
> *You should not be surprised at my saying,*
> *'You must be born again.' The wind blows wherever it pleases. You hear its sound, but you cannot tell where it comes from or where it is going. So it is with everyone born of the Spirit."*
> **"How can this be?" Nicodemus asked.**
> *(John 3:4-9 NIV emphasis added)*

---

* Nicodemus was a Pharisee, and if you've read any of the Gospels before, you probably know that Jesus and the Pharisees weren't usually on great terms. In a lot of ways, the way Jesus talked about God caused a disturbance in the way religion had always been done, and that felt like a threat to the Pharisees who made a living on things being done the way they were. So the fact that Nicodemus was willing to risk going to see Jesus at all, when they were supposed to be at odds with each other, was a big deal.

Okay, so we jumped into the middle of a conversation. And you're probably reading this going, "What in the world is Jesus talking about?" Well, Nicodemus was around for the whole conversation, and he was probably thinking the same thing. And what Nicodemus does here is huge. **He asks.** Nicodemus' questions don't shut him down and they don't shut the conversation down. They were used to move the conversation forward.

When Nicodemus had questions, he spoke up.

He understood who Jesus was and what He meant was too important to be misunderstood or ignored or silenced or brushed aside. The questions had to be dealt with for there to be any movement. And the same is true for you.

As you get started in your adult life, you owe it to yourself to

deal with your doubt.

That doesn't mean you have to have it all figured out, or have all your questions answered. It just means you don't have to stay quiet about what doesn't make sense, what bugs you, or what keeps you up at night.

In the story of faith, there's room for doubt and room for questions. It's possible to live with them *and* follow God with them. Essentially, **your doubt doesn't count you out.**

God isn't surprised by your questions. He's not disappointed in your desire for a better understanding of who He is.

Chances are, a few doubts have already popped up about your faith. So the question is, what are you going to do with them? It may seem uncomfortable at first, but dealing with them is one of the most faith-filled things you can do.

Here are two steps we think might be helpful.

1. **Acknowledge your doubt.** Like we said earlier, acknowledge it exists, but then talk to God about it. **That's why we're leaving the entire next page blank. This year, as you experience doubts, feel free to write them here.** There's no judgment. God isn't mad. And He's not afraid of where your questions will take you. He can handle it.

2. **Ask for help.** Who is someone you can talk to about your doubt? Is there a pastor, a parent, or a friend you can be honest with? Maybe no one comes to mind. If not, that's okay. Below are some ideas of the kind of person who is and isn't safe for processing your doubts aloud with.

DO look for someone who:

- takes your questions seriously
- empathizes with the challenges doubts can bring
- is safe and doesn't feel threatened by questions
- is honest

DON'T share doubts with someone who:

- gets angry when you challenge an idea
- brushes off your questions
- is scared of where your questions might take you

Remember, doubts don't have to be bad for your faith, but processing them alone can be. So **deal with your doubts** by inviting someone you trust into them.

I DOUBT IT . . .

....

....

....

....

....

....

....

....

....

....

....

....

....

....

....

Pray:
Share each of the doubts above with God. Even if one of the doubts is whether there is a God, it won't hurt to voice it. Remember, God isn't angry or disappointed when you have questions. So ask for His help with each one.

Deal with your doubt.

Have you ever had to change your mind about something? I'm not talking about your favorite slurpie flavor or your fantasy football pick. I mean have you ever had to change your mind about something *big*? Like which college to attend, or whether you wanted to keep dating a particular person, or whether *that friend* is really a good friend for you? If you've ever changed your mind about something big, you know it can be uncomfortable. We don't like admitting we may have been off base in what we thought or did in the past. This is true in lots of areas of life, including our view of God.

But this is exactly what happened to Saul.* As a Jewish religious expert, Saul was respected and well-known for his understanding of God. He would have been the go-to guy for teaching and defending his distinctly Jewish faith, which, at the time Saul lived, would have involved dismantling the teachings of Jesus because they were seen as a threat to Judaism. But then, on Saul's way to the nearby town of Damascus to do just that, something changed for him. Luke, the writer of the book of Acts, describes it this way:

---

*Saul is later called Paul in the New Testament as in THE Apostle Paul. Don't let the two names throw you off. It's the same guy.

*He went on his way until he came near Damascus.
As he neared Damascus on his journey,
suddenly a light from heaven flashed around him. He
fell to the ground and heard a voice say to
him, "Saul, Saul, why do you persecute me?"
"Who are you, Lord?" Saul asked. "I am Jesus,
whom you are persecuting," he replied.
"Now get up and go into the city, and you will
be told what you must do.
(Acts 9:3-6 NIV)*

Well, that was unexpected.

Saul gets stopped by a bright light and hears the LITERAL voice of Jesus. The same Jesus who was dead, buried, brought back to life, and then went to Heaven. *That* Jesus. The very Jesus whose followers Saul was trying to kill. Awkward, right?

When you have an encounter like Saul did, things change pretty fast. He realized if a *living* Jesus can speak to him, he may have been wrong about Him. And, that his understanding of God and His plan for humanity was off. Way off. Remember, Saul was a religious expert, meaning he wasn't just a show-up-occasionally-at-church kind of guy. He was SURE, until this conversation with Jesus changed everything.

We don't know exactly what Saul was thinking during those next few days, but we do know that he was temporarily blinded until he met a local believer named Ananias. Then, Luke says, it was like scales fell from Saul's eyes, the way Saul saw the world changed completely and he was baptized, and began preaching the message of Jesus, the exact opposite of what he was doing before. Saul changed his mind about God and ultimately changed his direction for his life..

At some point this year, you may need to . . .

be ready to rethink your faith.

Maybe you'll . . .

- **learn** something new that surprises you.

- **experience** something new that challenges your faith.

- **meet** someone new who changes your perspective.

What are some ways you've noticed your walk with God or your faith in God to be changing in this new stage of life?

....

....

....

On a scale of 1-10, how do you feel when someone or something challenges you to rethink your view of God?

Totally Uncomfortable   Totally Comfortable

1   2   3   4   5   6   7   8   9   10

How do you typically respond when someone disagrees or challenges your view of God?

....

....

....

It could be that we don't respond well to our ideas about God being challenged because we think God's highest priority is for us to know all the answers, have all the right information, and be 100% confident in what we think. God is so big and we are so small and our understanding of Him will ever only capture a small part of Him, which means the more we learn and grow in a relationship with Him, the more we will discover new things we may have never known before. This is true in any relationship—friends, the people you date, your family. So of course it's true with God.

Getting to know Him better means seeing Him more clearly and, sometimes, rethinking how we've always seen Him before.

Let's explain it a different way. In the letter we've looked at a few times already, Hebrews, the author writes,

> *For the word of God is alive and active.*
> *(Hebrews 4:12a NIV)*

The writer goes on, but that first sentence is all we need to look at right now. God's word is alive and active and when we begin to see God's word that way—and God that way—it will change the way we interact with Him. Because relationships with alive and active things don't stay still. They don't remain the same. They grow and change and we understand them differently at different times.

If you are alive, you will not stay the same. And that is true for your faith as well. So take a deep breath. If you think differently now than you did last year about something, that means you're growing. If you are uncertain about something now that you used to be certain about before, congratulations. That means you're alive. Change means life. It means you are still engaged with God and the world around you. In other words, if you are rethinking your faith, you are doing it right.

Don't let this freak you out. Actually, it should encourage you. By the time you graduate from college, chances are you are going to have some different ideas about a lot of things when it comes to your faith. *And that's okay.* You are alive. Your faith is alive. And alive things grow and change over time.

Just remember this: God doesn't change, but sometimes your understanding of Him will, and that's okay. So . . .

be ready to rethink your faith.

Now take some time to pray and ask God to help you see areas where you need to be ready to rethink. Be honest about the areas where you have questions and ask Him to help you know Him better and see Him more clearly.

Be ready
to rethink
your faith.

Have you ever heard the term "church famous?" It's the idea of someone being a kind of celebrity—but only within Christian circles. Like the super popular worship leader or camp speaker or Christian band. Ask anyone walking down the street who these people are, you'd probably get a blank stare. But at camps where these people are singing or speaking, teenagers are lining up for their autographs, asking for selfies, and waiting hours just to meet them.

Who are some famous Christians you know of?

....

....

....

Which, if any, do you follow, or keep up with?

....

....

....

There's nothing wrong with being a fan of someone or looking up to them, especially if they have helped you grow in your relationship with God. Although, maybe you've also noticed that sometimes it can go beyond just being a fan. (I don't want to say "social media stalker", but be honest. That's been you before.)

But sometimes all the enthusiasm we feel for being someone's *fan* is channeled into being someone else's . . . *not* fan. Meaning, we can have a tendency to take these Christian celebrities and make teams out of them. Like, if you follow this one pastor or leader then that means you can't be a follower of this other leader who disagrees with them. Or being a fan of this one group, or conference or movement means you are not a fan of another one.

This isn't a new problem. In the first days of Christianity, there were certain people who were famous among the earliest believers.* And, just like many of us, people began to pick their favorites from them. Similar to culture now, it caused some disagreements as people began to fall into one camp or the other, choosing one "Christian celebrity" to follow over another. In fact, here's what the Apostle Paul said in a letter to the early Christians in the city of Corinth.

> *For when one says, "I follow Paul," and another,*
> *"I follow Apollos," are you not mere human beings?*
> *What, after all, is Apollos? And what is Paul?*
> *Only servants, through whom you came to believe—*
> *as the Lord has assigned to each his task.*
> *(1 Corinthians 3:3-5 NIV)*

Even though Paul was one of the famous Christians of his time, he isn't flattered by the people "picking" to follow him. Instead, he points out that both he and Apollos are just human beings. And while they're teachers, they aren't people Paul's readers should fight over or follow blindly without question. For the next few verses, Paul goes on to

---

*A few of the people who knew Jesus, or knew people who knew Jesus, would travel from town to town sharing the Good News Jesus came to share. For example, Peter, Paul, Barnabas, Silas, Apollos, Stephen, etc, were on a sort of speaking circuit travelling around and preaching the message of Jesus.

write to the Corinthians about how he and Apollos and Peter (who he calls Cephas) are all kind of like farmers—some farmers plant, some harvest, others water. Or, they're kind of like construction workers with different jobs, serving different purposes on the construction site. Basically, Paul is saying Christian leaders are great helpers, teachers, or co-workers. They play important roles, but they should never become the figure-head of someone's faith. Why? Because they're not the ones we should be following.

In verse 10, Paul sums up the idea this way,

> *For no one can lay any foundation other*
> *than the one already laid, which is Jesus Christ.*
> *(1 Corinthians 3:11 NIV)*

Whether you follow famous Christians or just church leaders in your own community, Paul's words are true for us as well. The foundation of our faith is Jesus. His life, His death, His burial, and His resurrection. When we have Jesus in common, all the other things where we don't necessarily line up—like the kind of preaching we like, or the style of worship music we enjoy, or the any number of things that separates us from each other—don't *really* matter as much. In other words, we need to stop creating differences and sides and divisions when Jesus is what unites all of us.

It's okay to . . .

- learn from all kinds of leaders.

- listen to them.

- read what they write.

- sing their songs.

- like their ideas.

- agree with some of them.

- disagree with others of them.

But at the end of the day, **they aren't who we follow**, because they aren't what our faith is based on. And that means they aren't who we should fight about either. They aren't who we place our hope in or hang our opinions on. They're humans, just like us, in service to Jesus, just like us. So when it comes to church leaders and famous Christians, Paul is saying, **don't forget who you follow.** The guy who was killed and came back to life? He is the one worthy of our attention and energy. Not only that, He's the one we should take our cues from. When we listen to a sermon we should go back and check it's accuracy. We should test what we hear against the words of Jesus. He is our guide. He is our leader. He is who we follow.

When we can remember the place other leaders we follow should have in our lives, we will learn to become more generous towards those they are "fans" or "followers" of— even if we aren't fans or followers of them. It allows us to remember how important the essentials are that we share in common (following Jesus) and hold more loosely to the particulars of what that looks like—whether that's teaching style, worship style, fashion style or writing style. We can stop seeing the leaders we love and the leaders we don't love as being on competing teams. In fact, we can stop thinking of teams as being a thing at all.

Don't forget who you follow.

Be certain about Jesus. He's what matters the most anyway. And anyone who is leading others to follow Jesus is someone we can be a fan of, in some way or another. Don't create unnecessary divisions where there don't have to.

Who is someone (another Christian) who you have not been a fan of? How have you been harsher on them than maybe you should be?

....

....

....

What's one way you can be more gracious towards people you haven't always seen as being on your team?

....

....

....

What's one way you can remind yourself that, more than anyone, you follow Jesus?

....

....

....

Dont forget
who you
follow.

CLOSET
REMINDER

When you think about the kind of faith you want to have, there's a lot to consider. It's hard to narrow down the choices when there are so many and *everybody* has an opinion.

But what if it was simpler than you think?

When asked what was most important, or the greatest commandment,

Jesus replied:

> *"'Love the Lord your God with all your heart and with all your soul and with all your mind.' This is the first and greatest commandment. And the second is like it: 'Love your neighbor as yourself.' All the Law and the Prophets hang on these two commandments."*
> *(Matthew 22:37-40 NLT)*

Jesus said a lot there, but for now, pay attention to that last part. *All the law and all the prophets, hang on these.* Basically Jesus is saying, if you have a faith that gets this one thing right you will have the rest covered. It's kind of like buying a subscription to Netflix instead of renting individual movies (remember when people did that?). You basically get ONE thing and it covers ALL THE THINGS.

So what's the one thing Jesus commands us?

Love.

Specifically, Jesus mentions love in terms of three relationships.

- Love God

- Love Your Neighbor

- As You Love Yourself.

That's it.

It's *really* simple, but it makes sense. Chances are nearly everything you want to be in your life and your faith falls into one of these three categories. I'm just guessing here, but I imagine you want to be the kind of person who . . .

Loves God - a person of integrity, a person of faith, a "good" person, someone with love and joy and peace and patience. A kind person. A person with self-control.

Loves Others - a person who can be trusted, a good friend, a good boyfriend/girlfriend, a great son or daughter. Someone who looks out for others, leads others, and impacts others in a really positive way.

Loves Yourself - you want to be a person who actually enjoys your life, someone with confidence who isn't always trying to prove they're worth something, someone who enjoys the benefits of making good decisions.

In other words, most of the time **you and God want the same thing for your faith.**

Does that even seem possible?

Jesus underscores this fact in John 10:10 when He says *I've come so that you can have life to the FULL.* That means . . . a life with the volume turned all the way up.

- a life that is *more* than you expected.

- a life that is more interesting.

- a life that has more adventure.

- a life with more excitement.

- a life with more purpose.

It isn't that God wants something *different* for your faith than you do. He wants *more* for your faith than you do and it all starts with love.

CLOSET REMINDER

Go buy some clothing hangers. Spring for the wooden kind.
We know you're starting out in life but this is important.

You'll also need a dry-erase marker and a permanent marker.

1. Look back at the list of words you wrote on page ten describing who you want to be and who God wants you to be. Using the permanent marker, write one word on each of your clothing hangers as a reminder. Note: give it time to dry so the marker doesn't end up on your clothes.

2. Using the dry erase marker, write out Jesus' Great Commandment found in Matthew 22 on the clothing rod in your closet. You'll be able to remove it later so your mom or your apartment complex doesn't get mad at you. If the whole commandment doesn't fit, simply write Love God. Love Others. Love Yourself.

Once the marker dries, place your clothes hangers on the rod as a visual daily reminder that all you want to be and all God wants for you (all the law and the prophets) "hang" on loving God, others and yourself.

WHEN IT COMES TO MY FAITH

STARTING NOW
I WILL . . .

WEEK 04

INTEGRITY

integrity

[in-**teg**-ri-tee]

Definition: What *that guy*, who clearly hasn't showered or brushed his teeth since orientation, lacks. (Or wait . . . is that dignity? Eh, maybe both).

Definition: Something we all wish our ex had a little bit more of.

Definition: A character trait of someone whose beliefs and actions match up.

Definition: Something that's difficult to find, more difficult to become, and still worth it.

Definition: A trait that will define you and your years in college for better or worse . . . starting now.

So let's talk about the F-word.

No, it's not *that* one. For most of us, this F-word makes us even more uncomfortable.

Fake.

Is there anything *worse* than someone being fake?

When someone is . . .

Talking like someone they're not?

Acting like someone they're not?

Posting on social media like someone they're not?

Even if it doesn't hurt anybody, a lack of authenticity bugs us. And maybe worse than knowing someone who is fake, is when people think *we're* fake. It's insulting and one of the worst things we can imagine being called.

As insulting as that word is, most of us can think of a time when we've actually *been fake.* We've *all* been there and no matter what it was, one thing was probably true, it didn't feel good. When you're fake . . . you feel kind of gross about it. Even if it doesn't hurt anybody, even if no one knows about it, the thought of being fake feels wrong to us. **And just like this is true, the opposite is true, too.**

We love people who are real with us.

We love "real talk, "real friends" or being called "the real deal". When people act on the outside like who we know they are on the inside, it's just better. **We love real almost as much as we hate fake.**

Here's why this matters. The way we *feel* about fake-ness isn't an accident. Over and over Scripture reminds us that God is a God of truth, of light, and that He cannot lie.* And, as people made in His image, something in us draws us toward truth, toward authenticity, and toward real-ness. In other words, **something in us knows <u>who we are</u> and <u>what we do</u> should line up.**

What are some ways you've noticed that who you are (your beliefs, your values) and your actions line up?

....

....

....

What are a few areas where you've noticed your beliefs and values sometimes don't line up with your actions?

....

....

....

Uncomfortable, right? Something in us reminds us that what we believe and what we do *should* connect. And when they don't, we feel weird about it. James** put it this way:

---

* John 14:6; 1 John 1:5; Titus 1:2

** The brother of Jesus. Same James.

*What good is it, my brothers, if someone says
he has faith but does not have works? Can that
faith save him? If a brother or sister is poorly
clothed and lacking in daily food, and one of
you says to them, "Go in peace, be warmed
and filled," without giving them the things needed
for the body, what good is that? So also faith by
itself, if it does not have works, is dead.*
(James 2:14-17 ESV)

Basically James is saying something we already know—that if our faith doesn't change how we treat people, it's useless.

If we . . .

> attend church—but aren't kind . . .
>
> pray—but act like a jerk to our roommate . . .
>
> read the Bible—but act selfishly . . .
>
> lead a Bible study—but ignore someone who is hungry or homeless or hurting . . .

then our faith isn't really doing anything. You could put it this way. When we say we believe one way, but act another, we're being fake.

We may still be a good person. We may still be a believer. We may *feel* sincerely moved when we pray, worship, or read God's Word. But if what we believe doesn't line up with what we do, then there's a problem. It keeps our faith from growing, *and* it keeps our faith from being as influential with others as it could be. Faith needs work not to be fake.

Jesus made it simple. In one of His last conversations with His friends, Jesus said:

*If you love me,
you will keep my commandments.*
(John 14:15 ESV)

| 155

Make sure what you believe matches what you do.

It's the very definition of integrity. If we love Jesus on the inside, then we'll do what He says on the outside. And remember how Jesus summed up His commandments. It wasn't a long list of rules and regulations.

Love God.
Love your neighbor as yourself.*

Basically, Jesus is saying **if we love Him, we will love them—whoever our "them" is.** Our faith and our treatment of people are connected. Maybe for you, "them" includes:

- your sister

- your coworker

- your classmate

- your roommate

- your teammate

- your parents

- your professors

Take a few minutes and think of the people in your life, that you spend the most time around. Write their names here.

....

....

....

*Matthew 22:36-40. For more on this go back and read page 141.

Chances are, being loving towards your professor looks different than being loving towards your mom (or at least it should), but remember Jesus said love your neighbor *as yourself*. In other words, what would you want in their shoes? How would *you* want to be treated?

Think of each of the people you spend time with who you listed above. For each one, think of one or two ways you can love them by putting them first this semester.

When it comes to ....,
I can put them first by ....

When it comes to ....,
I can put them first by ....

When it comes to ....,
I can put them first by ....

When it comes to ....,
I can put them first by ....

When it comes to ....,
I can put them first by ....

When it comes to ....,
I can put them first by ....

When it comes to ....,
I can put them first by ....

Take a few minutes and pray for each of the people above and ask God to help you remember to love HIM by loving them.

Make sure
what you
believe
matches
what
you do.

Yesterday, we talked about how Jesus said the most important thing is to love Him and love our neighbor as ourselves. It's hard to argue with that. Nobody's going to be like, "I disagree. Hating everybody is *way* better." But at the same time, loving your neighbor is tricky. Everyone who's had a terrible roommate will confirm it. So what does it look like to put somebody first when they put you last? Aren't we supposed to have some kind of boundaries with people like that?

Who is someone that is difficult for you to love or put first right now?

....

....

....

How does the challenge to love them complicate your relationship with them?

....

....

....

Thankfully, most of Paul's letters* in the New Testament are about what it looks like practically to live out Jesus' command to love our neighbor. He takes Jesus' big ideas and gives us real application. And in Romans** chapter 12, Paul talks specifically about what it means to love other people. He says things like . . .

Honor each other (verse 9).

Be devoted to each other (verse 10).

Share with each other (verse 13).

Show empathy (verse 15).

Don't be conceited (verse 16).

It's basically "How to be Nice 101". But then Paul says something that gets to the heart of being nice or loving or kind when other people *aren't*.

> *If it is possible, as far as it depends on you,*
> *live at peace with everyone.*
> *(Romans 12:18 NIV)*

Basically Paul is saying no matter what we do, peace is the bulls eye we're aiming for. And notice what Paul doesn't say. He doesn't say:

- Live in *fake* nice-ness with everyone.

- Live as a doormat to everyone.

- Live being taken advantage of by everyone.

- Live pretending not to be mad at everyone.

---

* You remember the Apostle Paul, formerly known as Saul. Killed Christians until he literally met the resurrected Jesus on the road to Damascus. Then he became a Christ-follower and travelled from town to town instructing gatherings of Christians on how to live as followers of Jesus.

** Letter written to the Christians living in ancient Rome. They were most likely some of the first non-Jewish Jesus followers and heavily persecuted by the Roman government. The church most likely was made up of small groups that met around the entire city, where they would have circulated Paul's letter once they received it.

No, Paul says, as far as it depends on you, live at peace. *Real* peace. Meaning, don't fake it, and don't bear the responsibility of peace alone. You're responsible for your part, but sometimes it will be out of your control.

How would your life change if you pursued real peace (both in how you feel about and how you treat) everyone around you?

....

....

....

Chances are you'd feel less anxious. Less stressed. Less distracted. And, well, happier.

And that's what Paul's saying. In your life you can fight to be right, fight to be heard, fight to be nice or even just fight not to fight, but none of those have a payoff as good as peace.

So of all the battles you COULD fight, Paul is saying

fight for peace.

And remember, there will always be situations where peace isn't possible or doesn't depend on you, when you did your part, but nothing could salvage the relationship. Paul knew that and throws in the caveats of "IF it's possible and AS FAR AS it depends on you". Sometimes the only way to create peace in a relationship is to create distance between you and that person or even end the relationship. Obviously that's not what anyone wants, but if you've gone as far as it depends on you, it's okay to call for a break (or even a breakup) especially when those people aren't part of your family.*

---

* Of all the relationships in your life, we recommend fighting for peace (and the relationship) hardest with your family. Listen, we get it. Both of us (Gerald and Crystal) have complicated family situations of our own, but take it from us: they're ALWAYS going to be your family. Will you needa break sometimes? Sure. Boundaries? Definitely. But go as far as it depends on you to keep that relationship. When you graduate, get a job, get a house, get married, have kids . . . they're the people who will be there OR they're the people you wish were there. So fight for peace now so you can have peace later with your family.

Thankfully, those situations are the exceptions. In most of your relationships, peace is possible. So, what does fighting for genuine peace look like? It may mean you . . .

- let something go.

- bring something up.

- talk *to* them instead of talking *about* them.

- try to imagine their perspective.

- pray for them.

- spend less time with them.

- spend more time with them.

Living at peace with everyone looks different in every relationship. There is no "one size fits all" about it. But it's worth trying to figure out what each relationship requires and then doing the work to make peace happen. One way to do that is identify what the opposite of peace looks like for you personally.

What is your go-to fighting style? (circle one or two or five)

Yelling

Getting revenge

Arguing

Using Sarcasm

Being passive aggressive

Ignoring

Icing out

Talking about them

Pretending nothing is wrong

Beating yourself up

Winning mental arguments with them

Turn the book sideways and look at the chart below. In the following categories fill in who are you most likely to be at conflict with and what would it look like to fight for peace in each of those relationships?

Category	Name	What could YOU DO to fight for peace in this relationship
Family		
Roommates		
Classmates or teammates		
Friends		
Coworkers		

Take a few minutes and pray for each name you listed above. Ask God to help you see clearly what depends on you, what depends on them, and how you can fight for peace in that relationship.

Fight for

peace.

Have you ever seen somebody go on a power trip? Maybe it was a coach or a teacher you had in high school that was just a little *too* excited about their authority. Maybe it was a parent or step-parent who had an attitude of "because I said so". Maybe you grew up with an older sibling who actually thought *they* were your parent. No matter what the circumstances, when somebody in authority abuses their power (or just enjoys it a little too much), it's maddening.

That's why our relationship with authority can be confusing sometimes. On one hand, we're taught as little kids to . . .

- obey your parents.

- mind your teacher.

- listen to your coach.

- respect the police.

But on the other hand we've all seen people in authority who didn't deserve their position, their power, *or* our obedience. So what do you do with *that*?

In some ways, the Apostle Peter asked the same kinds of questions, only he did it 2,000 years ago. In terms of authority, Peter experienced the extremes. For three years he traveled with Jesus—the ultimate good, kind, and loving leader. But, Peter also lived under the unfair persecution of both Jewish and Christian faiths by Roman rulers who couldn't have been more cruel.* Knowing you should respect authority is one thing, but when you're living in fear for your life under that authority, it's something else completely!

Who are some leaders or authority figures in your life that are easy to follow?

....

....

....

Who are some leaders or authority figures in your life that can be difficult to follow?

....

....

....

When it came to difficult or wrong leaders, Peter had no problem speaking truth to power. Take a look at how Peter responded to the leaders of the Sanhedrin** after he himself was arrested.

> *Peter and the other apostles replied: "We must obey God rather than human beings! The God of our ancestors raised Jesus from the dead—whom you killed by hanging him on a cross.*
> *(Acts 5:29-30 NIV)*

---

* In John 18:10, Peter is so frustrated with the official named Malchus who came to arrest Jesus that he cut off his ear.

** The Sanhedrin was the assembly of Jewish elders or leaders. In ancient Jewish culture, they were the highest governing body and had big problems with followers of Jesus.

Peter didn't just confront his leaders, he called them out for crucifying Jesus. Talk about awkward. So why did he do it? Because what the leaders were asking of him was in direct conflict with what Jesus commanded. When it came to authority, there was only so far Peter was willing to go, which explains why some of what he writes appears to contradict other things he wrote.

> **Submit yourselves for the Lord's sake to every human authority**: *whether to the emperor, as the supreme authority, or to governors, who are sent by him to punish those who do wrong and to commend those who do right.*
> *(I Peter 2:13-14 NIV emphasis added)*

So, which is it? Do we resist or obey?
Confront or keep quiet?

The answer? Both. The reality is, there will be times when, out of respect for your Heavenly Father, you will need to disagree with or even disobey the people in authority over you. At the same time and for the *same reason*—out of respect for your Heavenly Father—we are called to submit to and give respect to authority. So how do we know when to do what? A few verses later, in the same letter, Peter sums it up.

> *Show proper respect to everyone, love the family of believers,* **fear God, honor the emperor.**
> *(1 Peter 2:17 NIV emphasis added)*

When it comes to authority figures of all kinds—including emperors and presidents, professors and parents, good leaders, bad leaders, and in-between leaders—the word that defines our relationship with them is, *honor.*

Obedience is one way to honor someone, and most of the time it's a good idea. (By this point in your life, you've probably noticed life is easier when you follow the rules.) Because even if you don't exactly love those in leadership, your life is just less complicated when you don't break the law, curse at the coach, ignore your professor or tick off your parents.

And in the rare times when we simply cannot obey, we can still honor those in authority by . . .

- speaking to them—and about them—with respect.

- hearing them out, even when we're pretty sure we'll disagree.

- refusing to make fun of them (even when they're pretty funny).

- honoring their requests, if at all possible.

As followers of Jesus, one of the most difficult ways we put our faith into action is by honoring *everyone*, because people won't always behave in a way that deserves honor. But that's on them.

Their actions don't determine our actions.

Their level of respect doesn't dictate ours.

We take our cue from Jesus, not them. And,

because of Him we can honor them.

When it comes to how we typically dishonor people, there's a spectrum. Maybe there are some people whose cars you want to key, and others who just cause you to roll your eyes. No matter the relationship, **what would it look like for you to take one step closer to honoring . . .**

Parents

....

Professors

....

Boss

....

Coach

....

Campus leaders

....

Government leaders

....

Pick one of the people on this list and spend a few minutes praying for them. Confess the ways you tend to dishonor them and ask for God's help in honoring them because of Him.

Because of Him we can honor them.

DAY **4**

Have you ever looked up the most-searched terms on Google or YouTube? Take two minutes and do it right now. Just search "most searched words". For fun you can add a particular year: like this year, your birth year, or the year you started eighth grade.

The words people search for can tell you a lot about what's going on that year in the news, pop culture, and the hallowed industry of meme-making. But imagine for a second that we could take the same technology and apply it to human beings. Imagine if you could type in your name and see *your* most used words for a given year.

Just for fun, what words do you think you've used most in the last year? (If you aren't sure, text a few friends and ask them.)

1. ....
2. ....
3. ....
4. ....
5. ....
6. ....
7. ....
8. ....
9. ....
10. ....

When it comes to the words we use most, they typically don't seem like that big of a deal. Well, sometimes they're a big deal. Maybe you know what it's like to spend hours typing and retyping a text message to the person you like. These words are a REALLY big deal. But for the majority of our day-to-day lives, we just don't put that much thought into what we say. And when you think about it, that's kind of weird because we actually care about words a lot. Chances are when you remember your proudest moments, biggest regrets, favorite memories, or really embarrassing fails, almost all of them had something to do with **words** you said or words someone else said *to* you or about you.

When you think about it that way, it's obvious words matter. And, in light of Jesus' command to love others and put them first, words matter even more, which is why, Paul says . . .

> *You used to walk in these ways, in the life you once lived. But now you must also rid yourselves of all such things as these: anger, rage, malice, slander, and filthy language from your lips. Do not lie to each other, since you have taken off your old self with its practices and have put on the new self, which is being renewed in knowledge in the image of its Creator.*
> *(Colossians 3:7-10 NIV)*

Paul begins by saying "you used to walk in these ways". In other words, this is how you were pre-Jesus. But knowing and following Jesus *should* change some things about the way you live *and* the way you speak.

Think about it this way: Have you ever watched a video clip where the sound and images didn't line up? It's maddening. Maybe, like us, you wondered, how is that even *possible*? In this day and age, we haven't fixed that yet? Preschoolers have their own YouTube channels now and most fifth graders can edit video. And yet, people still make videos where the speaker looks ridiculous because their lips are moving but the sound is something totally different and what's frustrating is the difference doesn't have to be huge to be noticeable. Even if the audio is just ONE SECOND off from the video, you notice. And if you're like us, you probably can't stand to watch that video for very long.

In a way, Paul is saying our words and our life with Jesus are kind of like audio and video, they should line up. One should be in rhythm with the other. When they're out of sync, even a little, people around us notice.

Listen, this is NOT about saying curse words versus not saying curse words. Paul is talking about something way bigger. Look at the things Paul talks about putting away:

> Anger
>
> Rage
>
> Maliciousness
>
> Slander (or gossip)
>
> Lying

Each one is about more than *which* words somebody used. It's about an attitude toward other people. It's a way of treating them. And Paul is basically saying, when it comes to our words (and our actions) we should get rid of anything that doesn't have the same attitude of Jesus, an attitude of love.

So how do you know if your words line up with the attitude of Jesus?

You watch them.
You pay attention.
You notice them.

Take a couple of minutes to scroll through the last few days of texts and DMs.

Give each conversation one of the following ratings in your own mind. Pay attention to the attitudes you hear in your words *and* how that attitude changes depending on the person you're talking to.

Based on your recent conversations, mark where you think the *majority* of your conversations fall on the following scales.

Complaining about people   **Celebrating people**

| 1 | 2 | 3 | 4 | 5 | 6 | 7 | 8 | 9 | 10 |

Gossip   **Grace**

| 1 | 2 | 3 | 4 | 5 | 6 | 7 | 8 | 9 | 10 |

Sarcasm (the mean kind)   **Kindness**

| 1 | 2 | 3 | 4 | 5 | 6 | 7 | 8 | 9 | 10 |

Negativity   **Hope**

| 1 | 2 | 3 | 4 | 5 | 6 | 7 | 8 | 9 | 10 |

Hate   **Love**

| 1 | 2 | 3 | 4 | 5 | 6 | 7 | 8 | 9 | 10 |

What are some ways you can remind yourself to

watch your words

and speak in a way that reflects the love and attitude of Jesus?

....

....

....

Pray and ask for God's help in guarding your words and speaking in a way that honors Him and them—whoever your "them" is.

Watch
your
words.

Our brains are fascinating. They can figure out how to keep us breathing, digest a burrito, *and* learn calculus. (Well, maybe not calculus. For some of us there's no hope with that one.) Our brains are also wired to help us find workarounds. If you don't have a pencil, you look for a pen. Don't have an alarm clock? Use the phone. Don't have tuition covered for this semester? Start a GoFundMe. Our brains are wired to use whatever tools we have to get what we want in the most efficient way possible.

And that's great. After all, where would we be if someone hadn't developed an app that gets food delivered to your door? (Let's all pause and give thanks for that brave pioneer). But our tendency to look for tools and shortcuts to what we want has a dark side. Basically, our brains don't always know the difference between tools and people. We all have a tendency to look at the people around us and notice ways they can benefit us. Like, if we play our cards right . . .

> the girl in class who takes great notes . . .
>
> the roommate with a fantastically full closet . . .
>
> the parent who doesn't mind doing our laundry . . .

have something that might benefit us.

And if that's not bad enough, our brains often do the same thing when we're dating, "talking" to, or hooking up with someone we're interested in. We think of all the ways that person can benefit *us*. Even more complicated, in college more than anywhere else, we're told to . . .

- keep it casual.

- not get too serious.

- experiment.

- hook up.

- don't catch feelings.

In short, when it comes to dating, culture tells us: **get what you need without getting too close.** In some ways, that makes sense. After all, there are dangers to a relationship getting too committed too soon. But the opposite— seeing people as a way to get what you want, as a tool or a product—is a problem. Because **when you see people like a tool, you'll treat them like one.** And that's the exact opposite of what Jesus taught when He said "love your neighbor as yourself".

Have you ever felt like someone was using you to get what they want? How did that feel?

....

....

....

But it's even bigger than that. When we treat someone like they're a tool for someone else to get what they want sexually, it doesn't just affect their current emotions. It also **affects their future.**

Maybe that sounds strange to you. After all, casual hookups are a real thing. And as far as we can tell everyone involved is *fine*. But fine isn't always the same as unaffected.

Because sex **isn't just physical**. It's more than that because *people* are more than physical. God designed sex to be physical, but it's also personal, emotional, mental, and spiritual. Sex is about two *people* uniting, not just two bodies—even if that's how we treat it.

It's easy to believe the body can be separate from the person and that sex doesn't have to have an effect on our emotional, mental, or spiritual health. But that isn't how God designed us to work. To use a term the writer of Genesis, Jesus, and Paul all used, sex is two people becoming "one flesh." It's everything—body, mind, and spirit—uniting together. Which means **there's no such thing as casual sex, no matter how casual people are about it.** You can't hook up and leave your soul, emotions, and mind parked outside. It doesn't work that way.

Not only that, we can't always know how our decisions now, affect us later. And **you can't know *now* how it will affect someone else later.** Culture may teach us not to care and that someone else's later isn't your problem. And we wouldn't be the first to think that. In an ancient culture where people often treated each other like tools or products for getting what they want, the Apostle Paul wrote the following in a letter.

> *Do nothing out of selfish ambition or vain conceit. Rather, in humility value others above yourselves, **not looking to your own interests but each of you to the interests of the others.***
> (Philippians 4:2-3 NIV emphasis added)

Paul wasn't writing about sex or dating here, but a mindset that works in every area of our lives. Jesus' life, death, and resurrection demonstrated "others first" over "self-first" more than anything else ever had before. And that's what Paul is inviting us to—as friends, as roommates, as families, and as people who are in relationships, even dating relationships, with one another. Jesus moved the metric from "focusing on what I want now" to "fighting for what *you need* later", and Paul encouraged us to do the same.

The truth is, sometimes sex in college creates a lot of regret and pain. And right now, in the present, we can't know how our decisions will affect someone 3, 5 or 10 years down the road. That's why we wait. Because we know having . . .

sexual integrity now means fighting for someone else's future.

In what ways are you tempted to think of people or treat them like tools that benefit you (in dating or just in life)?

....

....

....

How can you put others first in your dating life?

....

....

....

What are some ways you can remind yourself to fight for the future of the people you date?

....

....

....

Sexual integrity now means fighting for someone else's future.

MIRROR
REMINDER

Integrity sounds like a great idea, doesn't it? Becoming the kind of person whose actions matches their beliefs is a great goal. At the same time, you've probably already discovered actually living that way is a little more difficult than it sounds. If it hasn't happened already, some time this year you may find that you . . .

- said something you didn't really mean.

- messed up a friendship.

- crossed a line sexually.

- disappointed a parent.

- disappointed yourself.

- made a decision you wish you could take back.

The real question isn't whether some of these will happen. The real questions is, **what happens next?**

What do you do after you mess up matters—maybe more than you think, because it isn't just about what you do (or did).

It's about who you're becoming.

It's not just about the choices you made yesterday or the ones you'll make today.

It's about the choices you make **every single day**.

And that's good news because that means every morning you get the chance to start over.

Every morning, you get to decide who you want to be and how you want to live *starting now*.

This idea of starting over and starting now is so important that we want you to think about it, even just for one second, every day. And the easiest way to make that happen is to simply put a reminder where you can see it.

So, grab a dry-erase marker.
(Permanent marker will work, but you may not get the security deposit on your apartment back).

Head over to your mirror or your window and write . . .

STARTING NOW

Put that phrase somewhere that you'll see it every day as a simple reminder that yesterday's decisions don't determine today's direction and you have the power to choose a life of integrity every day, including this one.

STARTING NOW

WHEN IT
COMES TO MY
INTEGRITY

STARTING NOW
I WILL . . .

....

....

....

....

....

....

....

....

....

....

....

....

WEEK 05

FREEDOM

freedom

[**free**-*duh*m]

Definition: The feeling you get when you open an email with the subject line, "Class is canceled for today".

Definition: The ability to go out for burritos at 1am, write a paper at 2am, play video games at 3am, study for that quiz you forgot about at 5am, shower at 7am, go to class at 8am, and nap at 10am . . . all without getting in trouble—which is good because you're basically nocturnal at this point.

Definition: What you dreamed about in high school and what you most likely thought would be unlimited in college.

Definition: The thing that gets you in the most trouble but also is the reward for getting out of trouble.

Definition: Something God wants for you despite the fact that it feels like the opposite.

Definition: The ability to make decisions that will either increase or decrease the number of options you have each day— starting now.

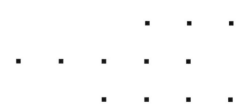

DAY 1

Have you ever had a friend date someone who you just *don't get*? Your friend goes on and on about this person's . . .

- good looks.

- great sense of style.

- brilliant intellect.

- stand-up worthy sense of humor.

But all you see is an average looking person with the personality of a vegetable. It doesn't make any sense.

That "what am I missing?" moment happens in a lot of areas of life and, for many of us, a lot of areas of faith. It can happen when somebody we know listens to or reads something and says, "This right here is game changing! Life changing! World changing!" Meanwhile we're over here thinking, "eh . . . I guess so?"

If you're like us, you've probably gotten that feeling after reading something from the Bible, like this one from Proverbs:*

---

* Many believe the famous king Solomon wrote or collected many of the wise sayings found in the book of Proverbs for his sons. Particularly in the first nine chapters, Solomon personifies wisdom and talks about it like it were a woman his sons, or younger men, should pursue.

Get wisdom, get understanding;
do not forget my words or turn away from them.
Do not forsake wisdom, and she will protect you;
love her, and she will watch over you.
The beginning of wisdom is this: Get wisdom.
Though it cost all you have, get understanding.
(Proverbs 4:5-7 NIV)

We get it. Wisdom is great. *But isn't this a little overkill?*
Maybe. However, when you look at the life of Solomon,
it makes sense. Solomon was born into a palace, a life of
privilege, and more freedom than we would ever know what
to do with.

Being son of the king, and then eventually the king himself,
no one was exactly lining up to tell Solomon ways he was
being foolish, or messing up or making stupid choices.
Solomon lived his life with total freedom to do whatever
he wanted.

Actually, you've probably thought about just how amazing
this life would be yourself. How much time did you spend in
high school dreaming about what college would be like? If
you're like us, you probably imagined . . .

- no curfew.

- no one checking your phone.

- no one asking where you're going or where
  you've been.

- no one telling you to clean your room.

- no getting grounded or yelled at or lectured.

Maybe that's what college life is like for you already, but even
if it's not, that's kind of the life you're headed for. Soon, if
not right now, you will have total control over your decisions.
And in that way, you have a lot in common with old Solomon

(Okay, maybe you don't have a palace or unlimited access to gold. But you do have freedom. So let's go with that).

And it's from this place of total freedom and total control that Solomon says the most important thing to chase, the thing we need most, is wisdom. *Why?* Because . . .

She will protect you.

She will watch over you.

After growing up in the royal family, Solomon understood something you may just now be starting to learn in this new phase. **Freedom is tricky.** Chances are Solomon grew up hearing the story of how his dad*, King David, used his own freedom as king to make good decisions and bad ones, decisions that would make him a legend and decisions that would make him a legendary failure. And when it was Solomon's turn to be king, he experienced the challenge of being wise with freedom himself. Because even though he had the *freedom* to do anything he wanted, he didn't always make decisions that kept the nation's best interests and his own long-term best interests in mind.

And that's what wisdom is all about: knowing what is good for you and good for those around you, now and later. And, it is the key to mature decision making as an adult.

When we're little kids, most of us have a single criteria for making decisions.

Will I get in trouble?

And as a little kid, that method works. The fear of getting in trouble most likely kept you from running in the street, playing in the garbage, or touching the stove. And in some ways, most of us take that question into our teenage years. We don't ask it the same way, but we do ask questions like . . .

---

* The famous King David (think David and Goliath, David and Jonathan, David and Bathsheba. You get the picture).

Will anyone find out?
(Will I get in trouble with parents or authority?)

Will anybody be mad?
(Will I get in trouble with my friends?)

Is it legal?
(Will I get in trouble with the police?)

Is it right or wrong?
(Will I get in trouble with God?)

Again, not *bad* questions. But Solomon is saying there is a *better* one. When you have freedom to make any choice you want, when you become a mature adult, you need a better standard than just, "will I get in trouble?" You need a better question.

And that questions is . . .

Is it wise?

Solomon spent his life discovering and writing down ways to answer that question because he knew, as a supreme leader, he would face countless situations with complicated circumstances and heavy outcomes.

Chances are Solomon understood something else about freedom. It isn't guaranteed . . . not even when you're king. The decisions we make with freedom now will almost always determine how much freedom we have later. No matter who you are.

It was true for David.

It was true for Solomon.

It was true for Solomon's sons.

And it's true for you.

Wisdom, as Solomon says, protects. And in many cases,

wisdom protects freedom.

When you develop the ability to make wise decisions, you'll find yourself with more opportunity, more choices, and even more control over your own life than you have now.

Lose wisdom and losing freedom isn't far behind.

What is a decision you're facing where you know for sure you need wisdom?

....

....

....

What are some areas of life where your decision is still based on the questions mentioned here?

....

....

....

What could be at stake if you make unwise decisions in college?

....

....

....

What would it look like for you to chase wisdom in those areas instead of just avoiding getting into trouble?

....

....

....

Wisdom
protects
freedom.

When it comes to junk food, nearly everyone has a weak spot. Maybe for you it's the perfect salty bag of chips. Or beef jerky or those tiny pizza rolls. Maybe you have a sweet tooth and you just can't pass on Oreo's or ice cream . . . or both at the same time. Whatever it is, we all have something that taps into our weak spot, our cravings. When it's around us, we just can't seem to *help* ourselves.

But our cravings are for more than just junk food, right? That "gotta-have-it-right-now" temptation can pop up in a lot of different areas. Gossip. Movies. Spending money. Sex. Porn. Alcohol. Temptation is everywhere. We're guessing you knew that already. The question is, because it's everywhere, what are we supposed to do about it?

Most of us know that giving in to our temptation never makes our lives *better.* At the same time, we're all well aware that saying "no" to a temptation is way tougher than it sounds. When it comes to temptations, most of us can quickly think of a few that seem to always come looking for us.

What are a few temptations that tend to get the best of you?

....

....

And while some of our temptations feel relatively harmless (hey, your arteries won't totally clog from all those Oreos for another thirty years, right?) other temptations just *feel* like a bigger deal. Sometimes it's because the consequences are heavier. Or because if anybody finds out, there's a bigger price to pay. But other times it's because we just feel powerless to stop when faced with them. We can decide to stop. We can plan to stop. But somehow, when that temptation shows up we end up giving in . . . again.

If that's you, you're in good company. **This isn't just a "you" problem, this is a human problem.** In fact, in one of Jesus' most famous messages, The Sermon on the Mount, Jesus teaches the people listening how to pray. And one of the lines in there goes like this:

> *And lead us not into temptation,*
> *but deliver us from the evil one.*
> *(Matthew 6:13 NIV)*

That's a big deal. This is THE example of a model prayer and temptation makes its way in. So Jesus obviously knew this would be something we would need help with. And I don't know about you, but that makes us feel much better. To have the Son of God teach us how to pray and include this idea of temptation let's us breathe a sigh of relief.

What we are facing isn't a surprise to Him.

And it is a great prayer to pray *before* we find ourselves caught up in temptation, but what about when we're in the middle of it and can't seem to find a way out? When our choices threaten our freedom? When temptation makes us feel powerless to say "no"? When we know God wants us to be free, but temptation makes us feel like anything but?

Thankfully, the Apostle Paul points us toward an answer. It shows up in a letter to the Jesus followers at Corinth.*

---

* Corinth was situated perfectly to be a hub for commerce by land or by sea. The central location meant travelers came to spend money and merchants came to take money. The city was filled with both wealth and misbehavior. Think Vegas . . . but ancient.

No temptation has overtaken you except what is
common to mankind. And God is faithful; he will not
let you be tempted beyond what you can bear.
But when you are tempted, he will also provide a
way out so that you can endure it.
(I Corinthians 10:13 NIV)

If we ever meet Paul, we're going to thank him for writing that first sentence. Because he drives home the same point Jesus does. Temptation affects all of us. And this is so important to remember because one of the worst tricks of temptation is convincing us that it's just *us*. That it's only *me* who struggles with this particular temptation. Paul says (paraphrasing here), "That's total garbage. This stuff gets everybody." It's nice to know we're not alone.

But look at the next sentence. You've probably heard it quoted (way out of context) at funerals when someone says, "God doesn't give us more than we can handle". That's exactly what Paul is saying . . . but not about tragedy. Paul's talking about temptation. We'll never have more temptation than we can handle because **He always provides a way out of it.** He always gives us an escape route.

Now that's not to say the way out is easy or that it comes with the very loud voice of God yelling in our ear to, "STOP RIGHT THERE!" But it does mean God doesn't abandon you in your temptations. He gives us a way out. Some ways are incredibly difficult. Sometimes asking for accountability or help or counseling to get out of a really tough temptation is the hardest thing we can do. But this does mean escape is always *possible*.

In the culture of Corinth, where it would have been easy to get trapped by poor choices, Paul is sharing the good news that they (and we) are not powerless. You are empowered. As a follower of Jesus, you have the freedom to say "no" to anything and anyone.

Including yourself . . .

. . . and your temptations.

So when it feels like you can't say no,

watch for a way out of temptation.

Because it's always there. God hasn't abandoned you. An escape route is available. Temptation doesn't have to get the last word on you and what you're future looks like.

Temptation comes in all shapes and sizes and genres. **What are some unhealthy things you're consistently tempted to . . .**

Think	Say	Do
1.	....	....
2.	....	....
3.	....	....

Which one makes you the most nervous (either because the consequences are heavy or you just feel powerless to stop)?

....

....

....

Chances are it's easy to see that temptation clearly right now while you're reading this book. But when you're in the moment, face-to-face with that temptation it can be much more difficult to see the way out. So, in order to see more clearly, try pre-planing for those moments.

When it comes to that temptation, what are some possible ways out?

1. ....

2. ....

3. ....

How can you remind yourself to **watch for a way out?**

....

....

....

Watch for a way out of temptation.

There are a lot of things that happen when a new semester starts, but maybe the worst thing is when you have to go around the class and tell everybody your name. Maybe that didn't happen in your classes this semester. If so, *you're lucky*. But if you began the semester by having to tell people your name followed by a candy, fruit, or movie that starts with your first initial? You know how annoying that can be. Even though you might have to spend the rest of the semester getting that one guy to stop calling you "Cameron Candy Cane" or "Taylor Tomato", most people aren't paying attention and they'll forget your name by the end of the first class anyway. And whether you've had to go through that same activity with hall mates or people in your fraternity or sorority, calling someone by a candy or something silly like that can help us remember their names, but it doesn't really help us know *them*. It doesn't tell us what to expect from them.

In new situations, our brains are wired to put people into categories and label them. That isn't necessarily a bad thing. Giving people a label in our minds helps us know what to expect from them. Maybe you labeled somebody on your hall as "the loud one" or "the fun one" or "the keep-your-distance-because-they-don't-shower one" (it happens). The point is, labels *can* be helpful. In our brains, labelling people is kind of the same activity as going to the grocery store and picking up a can or a box. We look at the label to know what to expect. If the label says "corn", we expect to find corn when we open it. If the bag says "Lime-flavored tortilla chips", we can assume that when we take the bag home we'll find the absolute BEST flavor of chip inside. What's true for our groceries is true of our friends, our classmates, and even *ourselves*.

Maybe you've never thought about that before, but we have a tendency to label ourselves just like everyone else. Sometimes the labels are positive attributes like:

- Hard worker
- Smart
- Good-looking
- Funny

Other times the labels aren't so positive. We're quick to call ourselves:

- Lazy
- Bad
- Ugly
- Loser
- Dumb

What are a few words (or labels) you think about when you think about YOU?

....

....

....

We get labels in all kinds of ways. Sometimes they come from what people have said about us. Sometimes they come from what society says about us. But maybe one of the most dangerous kinds of labels is when we label ourselves based on something we've done, making it who we are.

Maybe you . . .

- lied to your parents. And then you started thinking of yourself as a liar.

- did something stupid and started seeing yourself as a stupid person.

- failed a class (or just a test) and started thinking of yourself as a failure.

- slept with someone and started seeing yourself as . . . you get the idea.

Before too long you start to tell yourself . . .

this is just who I am now.

In other words, you did something bad . . . and eventually started to believe you *are* something bad. And that's why labels, particularly the negative labels we give ourselves, can be so dangerous. **Labels convince us that we aren't free to do something different because *what we did* is *who we are now.***

Maybe that's why the apostle Paul wrote what he did in a letter to the Jesus followers in Corinth.* The Corinthians, had gotten stuck in a rut of bad decisions one after another. And because they had lived that way for so long, there's a good chance many Corinthians, including the Jesus-followers, just saw it as part of who they are, that they would always be this way. And still, Paul reminds them . . .

---

* Remember them from yesterday? Vegas but ancient? What happens in Corinth stays in Corinth?

Therefore, if anyone is in Christ, the new creation has come: The old has gone, the new is here!
(2 Corinthians 5:17)

In other words, for those who follow Jesus, the old labels don't apply anymore. You are no longer defined by what you *did* or who you *were*. You are free to live differently. **And, you aren't just calling yourself something new. You *are* something new. *Starting now.***

In other words, you can

let go of your label.

For some of us that may be easy to believe the first time we mess up. Or if you made a decision to live differently at a church service or at a retreat or on a mission trip believing you are a new creation is easy in that moment. But then, you mess up. And then you mess up again. And before long you don't feel so new. It *feels* like the same old you doing the same old thing.

It feels like the old label fits so the old label sticks.

But Paul saw it differently.

Like a lot of Jewish leaders, Paul grew up hearing songs in the synagogue. And one of those songs that he probably knew and maybe even sang went like this,

"Because of the Lord's great love we are not consumed, for his compassions never fail.
They are new every morning;
great is your faithfulness.
(Lamentations 3:22-23 NIV emphasis added)*

In other words, you can't out-fail God's compassion and mercy. You can't mess up enough that it requires you to go back to who you were before because every time you fail, His compassion and mercy toward you are new again. And it's knowing that, that Paul writes we are a new creation. The old has gone. The new has come.

Every.

Single.

Day.

And that's why this idea is such a big deal. Because even if the old label *feels* true, you don't have to live like it is. You are free because you have a new one. You have a label that's not based on what YOU did. It's based on who HE is, who HE says YOU ARE and His faithfulness toward YOU. Your new label is . . .

So even if you messed up a thousand times since then and a thousand times after that . . .

Nothing you can do changes how He sees you.

You are HIS.

---

* The book of Lamentations is one of several books of ancient Jewish prayers and songs included in the Old Testament. This particular collection is inspired by God's faithfulness to Israel in times of trouble. As a Jewish kid, chances are Paul grew up familiar with those verses from Lamentations.

And, nothing you have **BEEN BEFORE** has to determine where you are going next.

You have the opportunity to be someone different.

And do something new,

STARTING NOW.

In what areas are you tempted to label yourself because of what you do?

....

....

....

How does that label affect . . .

The way you see yourself?

....

....

....

The things you say about yourself?

....

....

....

The decisions you make?

....

....

....

What would you do differently if you were sure that label was not true?

....

....

....

How can you remind yourself that you are a new creation, even when you don't feel like it?

....

....

....

Spend a few minutes in prayer and be honest about areas where you mess up over and over. Ask for God's help in reminding you that His mercy is new every morning and you can start over . . . starting now.

Let go of
your label.

Have you ever moved to a new place?

Maybe you've moved around a lot in your life. Or maybe your move to college was your first move ever. No matter what your experience has been, moving always involves some change. Whether you're still trying to figure out which light switch controls which light or what's the quickest route to school, figuring out how to live in a new place takes time. And even if you've never moved and you're reading this in the same bedroom you've had since you were five, chances are college still feels like new territory because there are still some quirks to figuring out how to live in *this* stage of life.

When it comes to moving or big change, there's always been an adjustment or a "figuring out" period. It's true now and it was true thousands of years ago with the ancient Israelites.

Whether you grew up in church or not, there's a good chance you've heard of (or watched Disney movies about) the leader of the Hebrew people, Moses. If not, here's the short version of the story.

For generations, the Hebrew people had been living in Egypt, until the Egyptian royalty, threatened by how large the Hebrew group had become, eventually made the Hebrews slaves. By the time Moses was born, they had spent so much time in slavery there's a good chance no one could even remember what it was like to live as *free people*. Slavery was all they knew. But then God uses Moses to lead the Israelite people from the foreign rule in Egypt towards a promised land where they can finally be free people again and live as a nation under God's leadership.*

Not long into their journey as free people, God gives Moses Ten Commandments for the people to follow. You've probably heard of those. They're easy to find and the things they command are pretty obvious. "Don't murder." "Don't steal." Nothing unusual about those. But for the Israelites, these might not have been so obvious. They had been under cruel leadership for so long, they had lived so long with someone else calling the shots in their lives that it may have been difficult to know where to start as a new society of free people. The old ways wouldn't work in their new world. So the Ten Commandments were more than just good rules to follow. They were God's instruction on how the Hebrews could live as free people.

But what's interesting when you read the list of Ten Commandments is the one that always seems to stick out a little bit.

> *Remember the Sabbath day by keeping it holy.*
> *Six days you shall labor and do all your work, but*
> *the seventh day is a sabbath to the Lord your God.*
> *On it you shall not do any work.*
> *(Exodus 11:9-10a NIV)*

Basically, God is saying, "Thou shalt take a day off". Strange, right? But remember, the Israelites were coming from a life of slavery with no days off *ever*. So to them, this law was unlike anything they had ever heard before. This was about more than having a day where they could sleep in. This was a reminder, each and every week, of how God was different

---

*The story of their rescue is epic. You should read it sometime. It begins in Exodus chapter 1.

than Pharaoh. God had compassion for them. God wanted to make sure they knew their wellbeing and their provision wasn't dependent on work, but on God's goodness towards them. Every day of not working was a time set aside to remember who God was, what God had done, and how God could be trusted.

And that was different than their previous leaders who constantly wanted more from them but never wanted anything for them.

When it comes to rest, we could learn from the Ten Commandments. Maybe an entire day of rest isn't possible, but just like the Israelites, you need to know that, **to be free you need rest.**

And **rest is about more than sleep.** It involves finding rest for your mind too. And believe us, your mind could use it. How do we know?

Netflix spends billions of dollars to have your attention.[4]

So does Instagram.

And every other social media app*.

Then there's friends and family and sports and campus organizations.

Oh, and school, too.

With everything competing for your attention, it can be tempting to let our minds work 24/7 and never give them a break. But if research is accurate, this kind of constant thinking doesn't make us smarter or more successful. In fact, it's the opposite.

For many of us, the idea of finding real rest feels impossible. Not only do our schedules and relationships compete for

---

* We don't hate Netflix or social media, by the way. We're actually big fans, but it'd be naïve to think they don't spend BIG dollars to keep our attention or that we shouldn't think about how they affect us.

our attention, but so does our faith. It can feel like, in order to please God, we constantly must do more, achieve more, work harder. But "work harder" wasn't the headline of God's message to the Israelites. It isn't to us either. Our faith isn't where we find more work. It's where we find more rest. Jesus clarified that message when He said,

> "Come to me, all you who are weary and burdened, and **I will give you rest.** Take my yoke upon you and learn from me, for I am gentle and humble in heart, **and you will find rest for your souls.** For my yoke is easy and my burden is light. (Matthew 11:28-30 NIV emphasis added)

Think about that for a second. You follow a God who wants you to **relax, slow down, and rest.** Your body. Your heart. Your mind. Your attention. Your emotions.

What part of you needs the most rest right now? (circle one)

Body   **Mind**   **Heart/Emotions**

What prevents you from resting in that area?

....

....

....

Spend a few minutes talking to your Heavenly Father. Ask for Him to help you relax and let Him restore you in the areas you need it.

Just like the Israelites, one of the best ways to find rest is to plan for it, to make a habit and

get into a rhythm of resting.

For the Hebrews, it was one day a week.

What could a rhythm of rest look like . . .

For your body? (Consider not only sleep, but exercise, or just changing routine.)

....

....

For your mind? (What are the things that demand your attention? How can you take a break from them?)

....

....

For your heart and emotions? (What relationships or situations keep you constantly worried, anxious or emotionally tired?)

....

....

How can you take a break from those?

....

....

Get into
a rhythm
of resting.

What would you do if there were literally *no* rules?

It's kind of fun to think about, right? No laws, no fear of getting caught?

Of course, some of us may have also seen a little film called *The Purge* and this whole conversation is giving us nightmares*. The point is, even if we appreciate the "don't murder" kind of rules, most of us aren't big fans of the everyday kind of rules. The "no speeding", "no cheating", "no skipping class" kinds of rules. And, in some ways, that's why **college and faith can feel like opposites.**

Most of us grew up with the idea that college = freedom. Obviously we knew there would be some rules, but compared to what growing up was like for most of us, college seemed like a vacation. So if you're going to break rules, push boundaries, make mistakes and create some great memories, college is the time for it.

But then there's our relationship with God. And at times our faith feels like nothing *but* rules.

---

* I, Crystal, have not seen that movie because the trailer (and all the ones that came after it) gave me nightmares.

We grew up hearing things like . . .

- Thou shalt not drink alcohol.

- Thou shalt not have sex.

- Thou shalt not wish you were having sex.

- Thou shalt not say curse words unless you only say the first letter or whisper them.

- Thou shalt not cheat (unless it's a take-home assignment. Then they were asking for it).

- Thou shalt pray and read your Bible.

- Thou shalt go to church and invite other people.

The point is, **it can be hard to see how rules and freedom go together**. College is a time for freedom, and faith seems like the place for rules. And let's just be honest. Freedom sounds way more appealing. In fact, that could be why you've seen some people you know or people you grew up with put their faith on hold in college, because there just didn't seem to be room for both. Maybe you've thought about it yourself.

If so, don't be hard on yourself. Christians have been wrestling with this idea of rules versus freedom since . . . well . . . since there were Christians. And that was especially true of a group of ancient Jesus followers in Corinth*. In a letter to them, the apostle Paul writes:

> *I have the right to do anything, you say . . .*
> *(1 Corinthians 6:12a NIV)*

* Yes. Same Paul. Same Letter. What happens in Corinth stays in . . . .you get it.

That sounds familiar, right? It's something we say all the time, even if it's usually in our own minds. Maybe as a kid you used to yell, "I can do whatever I want!" It wasn't true then, but it's more true now than it's ever been before. You can literally do *anything* you want. And I think Paul would agree. He goes on.

> *"I have the right to do anything,"* you say—but not everything is beneficial. *"I have the right to do anything"*—but I will not be mastered by anything.
> (1 Corinthians 6:12 NIV)

Basically, Paul is saying *you're right*. You are *capable* of doing anything you want. Especially by the time you're in college. But that doesn't mean everything you *can* do is good for you to do. Even if what you are doing isn't necessarily bad or wrong, it *will* affect you. Your choices now will impact your life now *and* later. And some choices, won't just affect you.

They'll master you.

Maybe that feels like strong language. After all, if you have the freedom to *do* something, you also have the freedom to *stop* doing it, right? Of course you do. Until you don't. We all know people who have used their freedom in ways that left them trapped, controlled or addicted. Again, that feels like strong language, but think about it.

You probably know what it's like to . . . .

- Procrastinate on homework for so long that your time is totally controlled at the end of the semester by trying to catch up.

- Say "yes" to too many things until your schedule controls you and you feel trapped by your own obligations.

- Become addicted . . . to the snooze button.

We've all been there. Here's why we bring it up. If using your freedom can lead to you being controlled in the little and mostly insignificant areas of life, the same thing can happen in more important areas too.

And that's exactly what Paul was getting at. He was telling the people of Corinth, you *can* do anything, but don't let anything become your master.

Don't let anything own you.

Why? Because you weren't made to be owned. The part of you that craves freedom was put there by God. It's part of His image in you. **You were made to be free.** And His rules aren't there to keep you from your freedom but to protect it and to keep you free now, in college, and for a long time after.

Why do you think God cares so much about protecting your freedom? What does that tell you about Him?

....

....

....

In what areas could your current choices lead to you losing freedom?

....

....

....

We aren't trying to pile on the guilt here. We just want the best possible future for you, and the best possible future is a *free one*. So we want to help you with this and set you up for the most success.

So how do we know if something we have chosen has already begun to creep in and take away our freedom? How do you know if you're being owned or mastered? It's easy. **The master makes the rules.** To find out if you're still in control of a habit or a pattern, give it some rules.

- Tell your phone it has a curfew.

- Tell your habit it's taking a month off.

- Tell your snooze button it's grounded.

The quicker and easier your habits obey you, the freer you are. The more difficult something is to stop, the more sure you can be it has taken some ownership over you.

What is one rule you will give to your habit or your choice to make sure you're still in control?

....

....

....

Is there any area where you feel controlled or like you've lost your freedom already?

....

....

....

Who can you talk to about that?

....

....

....

Listen, if there are areas where you're feeling controlled, trapped, or like you've lost your freedom, God's plan and desire is for you to be free. And, He has put other people in your life to help you get there. Tell them right now. Don't wait. Don't think about it. Text them or call them before you put this book down. If you aren't sure what to say, just take a picture of your answers to questions 3 and 4 and send it to them with the question "would you be open to talking with me about this?"

Don't let anything own you.

FAILURE
KIT

Freedom is great. But being free to do GREAT things also means we're free to do not so great things as well. No one is perfect and at some point you'll use your freedom in a way that you wish you hadn't. Remember in week two you said, **failing doesn't make you a failure?** But that can be hard to remember when you are in the middle of the failing.

What do you do, in *those* moments when failure isn't just theoretical but it's personal? How do you remember what Paul said? That there is *no* condemnation, guilt, shame when that's all you can feel in the moment? Well one way is . . .

plan to fail.

I know that sounds crazy, but let us explain. Paul reminds us that we *will* do what we don't want to do. We *will* mess up.*
That doesn't mean we stop trying to do the right thing. But it does mean, when we do fail we cut ourselves some slack, and still make sure not to let anything own us. How? We plan to fail by using the next few pages to create a failure kit for yourself.

Before you get started, think about this:

* See page 78

What are some areas where you might mess up this year?

....

....

....

What are some ways you may be tempted to give up or step back after you fail? (Ex. Skip out of church or being part of a faith community, stop praying, etc.)

....

....

....

With that in mind, write a letter to yourself on the next page. This is what you will read to yourself after you mess up. A few things you might want to include . . .

- Scripture verses to remind you what's true about you, regardless of what feels true at the time of your mistake.

- A reminder to yourself NOT to give up or back away from God when you fail (because He hasn't given up or backed away from you.)

- The phone number of someone you can call who will encourage you when you need it most.

When you finish, rip out the page, fold in half and staple it. Then, put it somewhere you'll see it if and when you fail.

WHEN IT COMES TO MY
FREEDOM

STARTING NOW
I WILL . . .

SERVICE WEEK 06

service

[**sur**-vis]

Definition: The act of doing your roommate's dishes before they start to grow some kind of fungal fur.

Definition: Letting someone cut in front of you in the Chipotle line even though you'd really rather not put another person between you and some chips and extra guac.

Definition: What you do for the community after too many parking tickets on campus.

Definition: Something that makes your life better, richer, and more adventurous.

Definition: The one thing that will make your college years matter more than anything else . . . starting now.

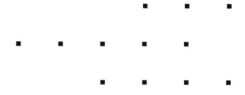

Have you ever been listening to someone and wondered, "What's the point of all this?" Maybe your professor was droning on about ancient forms of theatre. Maybe your roommate was telling you —for 15 never-ending minutes— about his trip to the gas station. Maybe your younger sister is on the phone with you right now talking about her friend group and you've decided to pick up this book. We all know what it's like to be in a conversation and wonder, "Is there a point to this?"

The worst is feeling this way about *life.* Maybe you sit in your classes and wonder what the point is of everything you're learning (I'm looking at you, War of 1812). Or maybe you wonder what is even the point of college at all? Sure you want to . . .

- get a good job.
- be good at the job you get.

But is that all college is good for? Is the point really just to get a job so we can use our salary for paying off our student loans? Or better yet, is the point of your life to get a job? Sure, jobs are important. We all like having food to eat and there's nothing wrong with making money. But chances are you have wondered if there is more to life than just a degree or just a job or even just a good paycheck.

There's a word for what we're looking for. It's called *purpose.*

Okay, maybe "purpose" sounds a little heavy to you. Maybe you're thinking, "I'm not interested in the meaning of life right now. I'm just trying to enjoy myself." Or, "I'm not trying to find purpose. I'm just trying to find a date." Or, "Purpose isn't my main concern. I'm trying to find some friends or find a way to pass my Lit class". In other words, maybe you aren't losing sleep over finding a purpose because what you really want is to just be happy. We get that. It's not weird to want happiness. That's what pretty much every person on the planet is after. **But what if we told you that your purpose and your happiness were connected? That finding one leads to finding the other? And losing one means missing out on the other?**

Maybe that sounds too good to be true, because you somehow got the idea that God's purpose for you is directly tied to *unhappiness*—like somehow the more miserable you are the more pleased (or at least impressed) God is. But what if it's just the opposite? We think it might be. Here's why:

In Ephesians, Paul writes:*

> *For we are God's handiwork, created in Christ Jesus to do good works, which God prepared in advance for us to do.*
> *(Ephesians 2:10 NIV)*

Before we get to the purpose part, take a look at the word "handiwork". Some people translate that word as "masterpiece". But either way, the point is the same. God made you specifically and on-purpose. You are not one of billions of mass-produced humans popped out conveyer belt style. And, you were not a random accident. You, your personality, your quirks, your talents, and even your

---

* The book of Ephesians is a letter the Apostle Paul wrote to the Christians living in Ephesus (modern day Turkey).

weaknesses all put together make someone completely different from any other person. God created you uniquely, *on purpose*, and *with a unique purpose* in mind.

Now, go back to the verse in Ephesians. The rest of the verse doesn't point to *how* you, this masterpiece or handiwork was made, but *why*. From the very beginning, God's plan for you was to *do good*. What kind of good? That's what you'll spend the next few years figuring out, so don't stress out if you haven't figured out the specifics yet. And, over your lifetime, the kind of good you do may change. But Paul's point is this: **You have been specifically created by God to do *specific* good things.**

Think about this for a second. Have you ever seen someone doing something they really love? Maybe it was playing a sport or an instrument. Maybe it was making a big group of people laugh or cooking or dancing or tuning up an old car. No matter what it was, chances are that person was pretty happy. It wasn't a chore or something on a checklist. It was something they *wanted* to be doing. That doesn't mean it was easy all of the time, or didn't require hard work, but there was something about watching them do what they were doing that made you think, **"it's like they were made for it".**

Something in us just knows what we were *made* to do and what we *love* doing somehow go together. Purpose and happiness are connected.

And Paul is saying,

you were made for doing good.

That is God's purpose for you. And even if it sounds crazy, that is where you will find the most happiness.

So what falls under "good works"? All kinds of things. But maybe the easiest, most clear way to define it is to say *serving*.

You were made to serve and in serving you will find the most happiness.

Now, maybe that doesn't feel true. A lot of us have tried serving before and it didn't exactly equal happiness.

> Maybe you worked at a soup kitchen and hated it.
>
> Maybe you volunteered at a trash cleanup day and afterwards were more smelly than happy.
>
> Maybe you tutored kids and they were really awful.
>
> Maybe you *had* to serve your younger siblings and it was irritating.

That's okay. There are a lot of areas of life that require some experimenting before you find the right fit. Chances are you didn't find your best friend the first time you showed up to school. You probably didn't find your "soul mate" on your first date. And maybe you haven't found your major, even though you're already in college. Nearly everything good in life takes more than a few tries to get right.

The point is this: these four (or five or six) years of college aren't just a waiting room until you discover God's purpose for you. They are a time for you to experiment with your gifts and talents. By serving others NOW, you're likely to discover even *more* things you're good at, a few things you're not, and the biggest issues you care about. As you do, it'll become even more clear that God made you on purpose and for a purpose. And, when you start to serve others according to His purpose, happiness is never far behind.

So, let's take a look at how God made you:

What are some things you've always been good at?

....

....

....

What subjects come easily to you?

....

....

....

What traits or skills do you get complimented on often?

....

....

....

What are some ways God could use the unique ways He wired you (that you mentioned above) to help the people around you right now?

....

....

....

What are some on-campus and off-campus opportunities to volunteer to serve others?

....

....

....

Spend a few minutes talking to your Heavenly Father and ask Him to help you see how He has wired you to serve the world around you. Then listen quietly to see if He brings something to mind. If you get no response or it feels like you're just talking to the ceiling, that's okay. Keep asking. Over time, God will help you see how you were made and how you live out your purpose *starting now*.

You were
made
for doing
good.

Let's do a quick quiz. Pick one class you're taking right now and answer . . . .

What time do you have to leave to make it to class on time?

....

How many absences can you have without failing?

....

What's the minimum amount of homework you can do and still get a good grade?

....

If you don't know, now's a good time to find out. That kind of information can come in handy. But we're guessing you have a pretty good idea. Why? **Because, as humans, we're all pretty good at figuring out the bottom line of what we have to do.**

And we don't just do this in class. We love to figure out:

> The speed we have to go to *avoid* a speeding ticket (Five over? Ten over?)

The *minimum* we have to pay to get a good lunch (Hello dollar menu!)

The amount we have to tip a server to still be a good person (15%. We're not kidding.)

Wired into our human nature is the desire to know exactly where "the line" is—what's the least or most of anything we can do/not do and still be "okay". Which maybe explains why in the middle of one of Jesus' most famous messages He says what He does. In this sermon, Matthew* records Jesus repeatedly saying, "You've heard it said . . . " and then quoting what most people would say they *had to* do based on the Jewish law or culture they would have all been familiar with. He talked about marriage and legal matters and conflict. And each time, Jesus flipped the whole idea upside down. For example:

> *You have heard that it was said,*
> *"Eye for eye, and tooth for tooth"*
> *(Matthew 5:38 NIV)*

In other words, when someone does something bad to you, you can do an equal amount of bad back to them. Not more. That was fair. That was expected. But then Jesus goes on to give examples of how we should do something completely different. Finally, He says,

> *If anyone forces you to go one mile,*
> *go with them two miles.*
> *(Matthew 5:41 NIV)*

---

* Matthew was a tax collector, which at the time meant "not a great guy". Despite his bad reputation, Jesus invited Mathew to follow Him. Matthew became one of the 12 disciples and eventually wrote down everything that happened during the time he walked with Jesus. The book of Matthew (the first book in the New Testament) is his own eye-witness account of what happened when Jesus was born, lived, died, and rose again.

In our context this sounds strange because no one forces us to go anywhere. But for the people Jesus was talking to, this idea of walking a mile with someone was all too familiar.

The ancient Jewish people listening to Jesus lived under the rule of the Roman Empire. And even though they accomplished a lot of amazing things, they also had a bad reputation for using and abusing their authority with unfair laws. One example is the law that said anyone over 12 years old could be forced to carry a Roman soldier's gear. Specifically, when commanded, they had to carry the soldier's gear for **up to a mile**. Imagine living in that kind of society where, at any moment, your day could be interrupted and you could be turned into a servant of the government. No warning. No consideration for how you were feeling or what you needed to do that day. It didn't matter how important you were, or how tired you were, when the soldier said "walk with me", you walked because that's what you *had* to do . . . or else.

Some people in Jesus' audience probably expected Him to say "don't go the mile. It's not your job" or, "Go the mile, because that's what's required". But most likely **NOBODY** expected Him to say go the mile . . . and then go another one.

The first mile was insulting enough.

The first mile was unfair.

The first mile was a burden.

And Jesus was suggesting they go a *second* mile? Why?

Because just like the unlucky one carrying the gear, the soldier knew what the person they asked *had* to do. The soldier would have known what was required. And watching someone carry his gear for a mile wasn't a surprise. It was law. It was what they *had to do*. But imagine the look on the Roman soldier's face when someone looked up and said,

"Can I take this another mile for you?"

Maybe he was shocked.
Probably he was confused.
But he definitely would have seen that person differently.

After the first mile, the person was free to go. So if they offer to stay, that changes the dynamic. And that is almost always what happens when you do something you don't have to do.

You've probably experienced this. Think about a time when someone did something for you they didn't have to do.

What happened?

....

....

How did you feel about it?

....

....

Most people are pretty good at knowing what we have to do or what we're obligated to do.

> If you're a roommate, you're expected to wash *your* dishes.

> If you're living at home, you're expected to do *your* part of the household chores.

> If you have a job, you're expected to do the parts of the job assigned to *you*.

But what if you did something unexpected? What if you did something *more* than expected? The people around you would probably take notice.

They might be shocked or confused.
They also might see you differently.
They might see the faith you represent differently.

Listen, we get it. This isn't a normal way to live. It's an inconvenient way to live. Growing up, most of us are taught to do what we have to do, follow the rules, pay our way, or do our share. And that's okay, you can do that, and be *fine*. But it's not the kind of life Jesus dreams for us. Instead, He has created us and called us to be different in the best way possible, to do more than we have to, go farther than expected, and leave a trail of surprised and changed people behind us as we go.

The second mile isn't about *having* to serve. The second mile is about *choosing* to serve when you don't have to.
And, even if you've never lived that way before, you can be the kind of person who does something they don't *have* to do, starting now.

Take a look at the chart on the next page. Use it to determine what you *have* to do (what's socially, academically, or legally acceptable). Then, think about what it would look like to go the extra mile and . . .

do something you don't have to do.

Area of life	What do you have to do?	What would it look like to do something more?
In your house/apartment/dorm		
In your classes		
In your job		
In your clubs/extracurriculars		
In your community		

The truth is, you probably won't be able to go the extra mile in every area, all the time. That's okay. You don't have to do everything to do something.

Pick one of the areas from the chart on the left and commit to doing that this week. Circle it and set a reminder in your phone so you don't forget. Choose to do one thing you don't have to do and watch the impact it makes on the people around you.

Do
something
you don't
have to do.

Depending on what app you're using there's probably thousands, if not millions, of songs available to you right now. Spotify alone has enough music that you could listen **FOR THE REST OF YOUR LIFE** and never repeat a song*. We have endless options at our fingertips. And yet, every year people spend billions of dollars to leave their house, stand in line, push through a crowd to hear the *exact same music* at a live show. Why?

Because concerts are awesome.

Maybe it's seeing your favorite artist up close. Maybe it's the vibe of being in a crowd who all shout the lyrics at the same time. Or maybe it's the feeling in the moment when everyone gets out their phone flashlights.

You know what we're talking about. There's always a point in the show where people turn on their flashlights and wave them in the air when it looks like a thousand tiny points of light in the room. And even though each point of light is *minuscule* compared to the size of the room, you can see every single one of them. Even if there was just one, you could still see that single light, no matter how dark the room. That's what makes light different than nearly every other force in the universe.

---

* OK, we made that statistic up, but it seems pretty reasonable, right?

And, maybe that's why Jesus talked about it so much. Over and over, when making a point, Jesus would compare light and darkness. One of those times was recorded by Matthew in the same sermon we looked at yesterday. As a large crowd listened, Jesus explained how His followers should live differently, *very* differently than expected. Then, in the middle of the sermon, He says . . .

> *You are the light of the world. A town built on a hill cannot be hidden. Neither do people light a lamp and put it under a bowl. Instead they put it on its stand, and it gives light to everyone in the house. In the same way, let your light shine before others, that they may see your good deeds and glorify your Father in heaven.*
> *(Matthew 5:14-16 NIV)*

There's nothing complicated about what Jesus is saying here.

Light is good.

Light should never be hidden.

The interesting part isn't how Jesus describes light, though. In fact, this conversation isn't even really about light at all. Look at the first line:

YOU are the light of the world.

This passage isn't about lamps, even though that's the image Jesus mentions. It's about *you*. And specifically, it's about you living in a way that . . .

- others notice.

- others pay attention to.

- and others connect to your Father in Heaven.

In other words, it's about YOU deciding to

live in a way that lights the way.

Maybe that sounds a little strange. Sure, you can follow the light, but you've never really considered yourself a light that others follow. Maybe you've always felt like God used other people, expert-level people, Christian club leader people, or professional pastor-people. But notice that Jesus never said, "let your light shine *when* others are watching "or" *if* others are watching." No, Jesus just assumes others are watching.

Why?

Because you can't *not* see light in a dark room.

Even in a dark movie theatre, you notice when one person turns on their phone. Because light stands out in the dark. Even if you aren't looking for it, you are drawn to it. You pay attention to it. And that's true for you too. If you shine, others will notice. And that's a big deal because the world can be a really dark place. You know this. You know this from catching pieces of the news, to scrolling through social media, to your own personal experience. There's scary stuff happening in the world, and overwhelming stuff happening in *your* world. And you aren't the only one who feels that way. Everyone around you is trying to come to terms with how big and anxiety producing and overpowering the world can feel.

In other words, everyone is looking for a little bit of light. And when the world is as dark as it is, **you can live in a way that lights the way towards a Heavenly Father who loves them.** You don't have to be an expert or a professional or anything else besides who you already are. You just have to be light.

So how exactly do you live as light? Jesus is very specific when He says, "they may see your good deeds". We are a light in the darkness around us when we serve in a way that makes those around us pay attention. Our *goodness* is a light.

Maybe that means you:

- **Serve your friends** by always showing up for them when they need it, refusing to talk bad about them, encouraging them, or looking out for them.

- **Serve your community** by finding a place to volunteer and serve those in need, then showing up consistently so you can be counted on.

- **Serve the world** by signing up for a short term or even a long-term mission trip or relief effort. Or, support someone who does.

Just like there are thousands of different kinds of light (flashlights, matches, lighters, lamps, nightlights, tablet screens just to name a few) there are tons of ways that you can live in a way that's a light for those around you.

The only thing you really have to be is different than the darkness.

Think about someone who has been a light in the darkness for you.

What did you notice about them?
How did their actions point you to God?

....

....

....

What are some ways you can decide
this week **be a light . . . .**

In your friend group?

....

....

In your community?

....

....

In the world?

....

....

**Who is one person that might notice or be affected if you
chose to live in a way that lights the way?**

....

....

....

Take a few minutes to pray for that person. Ask God to use
you to light the way from them to Him.

Live in
a way
that lights
the way.

Think back to when you were a kid.
Who did you look up to?

Maybe you were a huge fan of professional wrestlers or pro athletes. Maybe it was a celebrity or a musical artist. Or maybe it was someone you knew personally— an older kid you thought was cool and wanted to be like or a sibling you constantly annoyed but secretly worshipped. We all have those people we want to grow up and be like. And, when you're young, there is just something about people slightly older than you that makes them seem cooler, smarter, and more role-model worthy.

No matter who *that* person was for you when you were young, there was also most likely someone you looked up to, not because of their age or their haircut or their sports ability, but because of their faith. Chances are, somewhere there is a person of faith, a Jesus-follower, a role-model who impacted you. And that's what makes this passage from Hebrews on the next page especially practical at this stage of your life. If you've ever been influenced or impacted by someone who taught you about Jesus, the author of Hebrews has something to say that could radically impact the next few years for you.

It begins in chapter 13.

Remember your leaders,
those who spoke the word of God to you.
(Hebrews 13:7 NIV emphasis added)

Whether that was a Sunday School teacher, a pastor, a youth pastor, a small group leader, a high school teacher, a parent, an uncle or aunt, a sibling, or an older friend who made a positive impact on you, **write their names here.***

....

....

....

The letter goes on:

Consider the outcome *of their way of life.*

So, what is the outcome of the person you listed above? Put simply, *you*. You are. Your faith, your wisdom, the way you see the world, those are all outcomes of "their way of life". Below, **write a few ways you benefitted personally from the people you listed above.** (Things they taught you, modeled for you, or encouraged you about.)

....

....

....

The letter continues with the real kicker . . .

Imitate *their faith*
(Hebrews 13:7 NIV emphasis added)

* And if you want to make their day, snap a photo of this page and text it to them.

That's kind of a big ask. To *imitate*. We get it. But, this isn't necessarily about imitating their prayer habits or devotional time (even though they may not be a bad idea). Faith, by definition, is *confidence*. It's trust that God is doing something good, even when you can't *see* what He is doing. And that's what the person who lead you did. They had great *faith*.

Think about it: **it took a lot of *faith* to lead you.** At the time, they couldn't see the outcome of their time with you. When the people you listed above were spending time with you, praying for you, hanging out with you, they couldn't *see* you, years later, sitting down and doing a college devotional. Chances are, what they saw, was everything they had to do in order to lead you:

- Make a weekly commitment to showing up.

- Take time off work for a church camp or retreat.

- Stay up late to talk you through some stuff.

- Hang out with someone younger than them in their free time.

That doesn't mean they were miserable. Whoever lead you probably *loved* it, but it was because they had faith that God was using their time with you to do something meaningful in your life. They had faith that their time spent would be *worth* it in the end.

And look at that . . . they were right.

The point is, someone, somewhere did something for you that made your life better. *And you can do the same.* You have the opportunity to imitate that person's faith by doing exactly what they did—investing in the next generation.

It may be hard to imagine affecting the fate of the next generation while you're still trying to figure out how to survive in college. Maybe you still feel like you ARE the next generation. Maybe you simply wonder if you have what it takes to lead someone younger than you toward God.

The good news is you have *exactly* what it takes. In a word? You have *influence*. Simply because you're a little older, with more life experience you have more influence with people a little bit younger than you.

When *you* talk? They're more likely to listen.

When *you* ask questions?
They're more likely to answer.

And when *you* make decisions? They'll be watching and they're more likely to follow your lead.

This isn't about just volunteering or encouraging or hanging out with kids or teenagers. It's about investing in them and having influence in their lives. This is about playing a leading role in someone's life story.

Imagine this for a second. If you had the chance to invest in someone younger than you, someone who looked up to you, what would you say to them? What would you hope they learn from you?

....

....

....

Whether you have thought about signing up to be a mentor, a small group leader, a coach, or a Sunday School teacher, college is one of the *best* times in your life to become the kind of person someone else looks up to.

BUT . . . there's a catch.

Influence isn't something that happens the first time you meet somebody. We're guessing you know this already. The person you mentioned at the the beginning of this section, the one who had an impact on your life probably wasn't somebody that you only saw one time or a handful of times. **The people that have the most impact in our lives show up for us and they *keep* showing up.** And that means if we want to imitate their faith, if we want to have the kind of impact they had, we have to become the kind of people who *consistently* show up in the lives of people younger than us.

One of the best ways to do that is deciding to volunteer weekly at a local church in their kid's ministry or student ministry areas. But no matter where you sign up to serve, we want you to keep this in mind:

Influencing someone and *feeling like* you're influencing someone are different.

There will be days when it doesn't feel like you're accomplishing much, or it feels like a waste of time. It isn't. If you sign up to serve somewhere regularly, you'll make an impact *over time* that you couldn't have imagined *at the time* you were making it. So sign up anyway. Show up anyway. Commit to being a part of someone's life *consistently* and then . . .

set your schedule to serve the next generation.

Just like your *leader*, you'll be glad you did.

What are some consistent ways you could sign up to serve people younger than you consistently?

HOW I COULD SERVE	WHERE I COULD SERVE	WHEN I COULD SERVE
Small group leader, sports coach, kids greeter team, young-life leader, Sunday School teacher, student ministry tech team etc.	(name the exact church or organization)	Take a few moments to estimate the days or times required each week to serve in this area.

What might you have to sacrifice to serve in this way?

....

....

....

What might you miss out on if you choose *not* to serve in this way?

....

....

....

Spend a few minutes asking God for wisdom in how and where and when you can serve the next generation. Then, ask for the courage to do whatever it is that He calls you to do.

Set your schedule to serve the next generation.

What's your go-to time-waster? (No judgment. We all have one.) Go ahead and write it here.

....

....

....

Maybe you start a Netflix show and look up 3 seasons later and you're still on the couch. Maybe you get sucked into Insta-scrolling when you're supposed to be studying or you watch perfectly meaningless YouTube videos (hello ASMR. We're looking at you) for hours to avoid reading for your Lit class.

The point is, we all have a go-to *something* we use to avoid the other less-desirable *somethings* in our lives. We all have a favorite way (or five) to waste time. And for the most part, it all feels pretty harmless.

At the same time, we're guessing you know somebody who wastes money. We all have that friend who makes us raise our eyebrows with their purchases. The point is, when someone seems to be spending a lot of money, or *wasting* money, we notice. And most of us notice for the same reason:

Our money is limited.

If we spend $20 on candy at the gas station that means we may not have the money we need later to buy gas. But for some reason that's hard to keep in mind when it comes to how we spend our time.

I think that's why, in Psalm 90, Moses* points out how important it is to pay attention to our time, writing,

> Teach us to number our days,
> that we may gain a heart of wisdom.
> (Psalm 90:12 NIV)

Basically, Moses realizes two very important things:

1. Time isn't unlimited.
2. We all tend to forget time isn't unlimited.

Moses asks God to help him remember how much time is passing. Why? Because Moses understands, a healthy view of the time we have left is directly connected to how much wisdom we possess.

At the time Moses writes this he was leading God's people, who for their entire lives had been slaves. Now they were free. And Moses is saying, to a group of people with boundless possibilities, "Just because there's no one to tell you what to do, doesn't mean you shouldn't have a plan for the days you have."

Moses's words are for us too. In a time when you have more freedom than you have ever had before, you have to figure out how to make the most of what you have, because you *can't make more time.* And while you and I are free to spend our time however we want, it'd be wise to

---

* Remember the movie Prince of Egypt? Ok, it may have not been entirely accurate, but that's the same Moses we're talking about. Called by God to defy Pharaoh and lead his people to freedom. Also, the guy God gave the Ten Commandments to.

never waste what you can't replace.

Here's what we mean.

The average life span in North America is between 76 and 81 years old. Let's be optimists and say you'll live to be 80. Then,

WRITE YOUR
AGE HERE

 $\div\ 80 =$

Lose the decimal and that's the percent of your life *you've already lived.*

STARTLING, isn't it?

When we realize how quickly time passes, suddenly it's easier to . . .

- skip the next episode.

- log-off YouTube.

- delete the app that wastes the most time.

- do the thing you've been putting off.

- do whatever it takes to make the next minute, day, week, year count.

Because when we pay attention to the time we have left, we do more with the time we have now.[5]

So what do you want to do with your time here?

How do you want your story to go? What do you want to be known for or remembered for?

It's an important question because your life doesn't start when you leave college. You're living it right now. And, only *you* get to decide what you'll do with your time here.

Just a few days before Jesus was crucified and eventually raised from the dead, He faced a similar question. Toward the end of his account, John* records it this way,

> *It was just before the Passover Festival.*
> *Jesus knew that the hour had come for him to*
> *leave this world and go to the Father.*
> *(John 13:1 NIV)*

In other words, Jesus knew His time was limited and He was paying attention. John doesn't tell us what Jesus was thinking about, but we can imagine, like us, Jesus wanted to make the most of the time He had left.

In that moment, He could have done anything. So what did He do? He grabbed a towel, knelt down, and began to wash the feet of those around Him. In that society, foot-washing was common, but it was the duty of servants, not teachers, and definitely *not* the Son of God. The Son of God, with limited time left **chose to serve.**

---

* John walked with Jesus and was one of His closest friends. Eventually, John wrote down his eye-witness account of what Jesus did and what He was like. This account is called the Gospel of John and is included alongside three-other accounts of Jesus' life at the beginning of the New Testament.

John continues,

> *When he had finished washing their feet,*
> *he put on his clothes and returned to his place.*
> *"Do you understand what I have done for you?" he*
> *asked them. "You call me 'Teacher' and 'Lord,' and*
> *rightly so, for that is what I am. Now that I, your Lord*
> *and Teacher, have washed your feet, you also should*
> *wash one another's feet. I have set you an example*
> *that you should do as I have done for you.*
> *(John 13:12-15 NIV)*

Jesus, in His wisdom, used His limited time to create unlimited impact. He used His time to serve. And, He reminds us that, if we are to follow Him, if we want to make the most of the time we have, we will do the same.

He invites us into a story of hope.
A story of redemption.
A story that has changed and is changing the world.
A story we participate in by serving the people around us.

The best news is that story is *starting now*. And we can do it starting small. We begin by numbering our days. And then we live in a way that optimizes the time we have left.

When your college years are over, what do you hope to be known for or remembered for?

....

....

....

What would it look like for you to use your college years to impact people the way Jesus impacted you?

....

....

....

What is one thing you need to do STARTING NOW to make the most of your college years?

....

....

....

Never
waste what
you can't
replace.

WHEN IT
COMES TO MY
SERVICE

STARTING NOW
I WILL . . .

STARTING
NOW
MANIFESTO

Remember those pages you've been filling out at the end of each week? The ones that say:

When it comes to . . . .

Starting now, I will . . . .

As you come to the end of this book we want you to take out those pages (including the page following this) and staple them all together. THIS is your Starting Now manifesto.

Over the next couple of months as you continue to settle in to this new stage of life, pull out your manifesto every now and then and remember the decisions you've made. In fact, **go ahead and schedule it.** Take a second and put a reminder in your phone for mid-terms and finals week to pull out this collection of decisions and check in.

Every time you do, read this:

No matter what yesterday was like, starting now you can begin to move in the direction towards community, healthy identity, faith, integrity, freedom, and service. It's never too late to start. And it's never too late to start again.

STARTING NOW
MANIFESTO

**No matter what yesterday was like,
starting now you can begin to**

**move in the direction towards community,
healthy identity, faith, integrity, freedom,
and service. It's never too late to start.**

And it's never too late to start again.

Endnotes

1 Bureau of Labor Statistics. "America's Young Adults at 27: Labor Market Activity, Education, and Household Composition: Results from a Longitudinal Survey." BLS.gov, April 8, 2016. http:// www. bls.gov/news.release/nlsyth.nr0.htm

2 https://www.huffingtonpost.ca/2017/07/14/85-of-jobs-that-will-exist-in-2030-haven-t- been-invented-yet-d_a_23050098/

3 https://www.businesswire.com/news/home/20181005005380/en/U.S.-Health-Coaching- Market-2018-Emerged-6

4 We're pretty sure our boss wrote that. Let's give him credit. Thanks Reggie!

5 https://www.cnbc.com/2018/01/23/netflix-2018-marketing-budget-to-hit-2-billion.html

MORE FROM
GERALD FADAYOMI

Life is constantly changing, and with every new season comes a new set of challenges.

As you prepare to leave high school behind and move into a new season, this book will serve as a guide to help you maintain and grow your faith in college. In the pages of this short book you'll find letters from college freshman, ten ideas that will help prepare you for what's ahead, and questions to help you process and apply what you've read.

www.OrangeStore.org

MORE FROM
CRYSTAL CHIANG

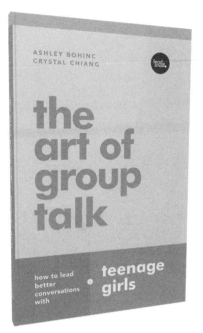

**Sometimes people talk too much—way too much.
Sometimes they don't talk enough.**

So if you've ever wished you knew what to say, what not to say, when to speak, when to listen, how to make others talk, or how to make them stop talking, then The Art of Group Talk is for you. These books can remind you that your small group conversations—even the ones that don't go exactly as planned—really matter. But there are a few ways to make your conversations matter even more.

The Art of Group Talk is part of a series of books for leaders of kids, teenage girls, and teenage guys.

www.OrangeStore.org